Cultures and Change in Education

CW00661471

Universities into the 21st Century

Series Editors: Noel Entwistle and Roger King

Paul Trowler
CULTURES AND CHANGE IN HIGHER EDUCATION

Wyn Grant with Philippa Sherrington
MANAGING YOUR ACADEMIC CAREER

Angela Brew
RESEARCH AND TEACHING

Lisa Ganobcsik-Williams (editor)
TEACHING ACADEMIC WRITING IN UK HIGHER EDUCATION

Roger King
THE UNIVERSITY IN THE GLOBAL AGE

Noel Entwistle
UNIVERSITY TEACHING AND STUDENT LEARNING

Further titles are in preparation

Also by Paul Trowler

REALISING QUALITATIVE RESEARCH IN HIGHER EDUCATION (*co-editor with Prichard, C.*)

EDUCATION POLICY: A Policy Sociology Approach (2nd edition)

HIGHER EDUCATION POLICY AND INSTITUTIONAL CHANGE: Intentions and Outcomes in Turbulent Environments (*editor*)

ACADEMIC TRIBES AND TERRITORIES: Intellectual Enquiry and the Cultures of Disciplines (2nd edition) (*with Becher, T.*)

DEPARTMENTAL LEADERSHIP IN HIGHER EDUCATION: New Directions for Communities of Practice (*with Knight, P.*)

ACADEMICS RESPONDING TO CHANGE: New Higher Education Frameworks and Academic Cultures

Cultures and Change in Higher Education

Theories and Practices

Paul Trowler

© Paul Trowler 2008

All rights reserved. No reproduction, copy or transmission of this publication may be made without written permission.

No paragraph of this publication may be reproduced, copied or transmitted save with written permission or in accordance with the provisions of the Copyright, Designs and Patents Act 1988, or under the terms of any licence permitting limited copying issued by the Copyright Licensing Agency, 90 Tottenham Court Road, London W1T 4LP.

Any person who does any unauthorized act in relation to this publication may be liable to criminal prosecution and civil claims for damages.

The author has asserted his right to be identified as the author of this work in accordance with the Copyright, Designs and Patents Act 1988.

First published 2008 by
PALGRAVE MACMILLAN
Houndmills, Basingstoke, Hampshire RG21 6XS and
175 Fifth Avenue, New York, N.Y. 10010
Companies and representatives throughout the world

PALGRAVE MACMILLAN is the global academic imprint of the Palgrave Macmillan division of St. Martin's Press, LLC and of Palgrave Macmillan Ltd. Macmillan® is a registered trademark in the United States, United Kingdom and other countries. Palgrave is a registered trademark in the European Union and other countries.

ISBN-13: 978–1–4039–4853–3
ISBN-10: 1–4039–4853–4

This book is printed on paper suitable for recycling and made from fully managed and sustained forest sources. Logging, pulping and manufacturing processes are expected to conform to the environmental regulations of the country of origin.

A catalogue record for this book is available from the British Library.

A catalog record for this book is available from the Library of Congress.

10   9   8   7   6   5   4   3   2   1
17   16   15   14   13   12   11   10   09   08

Printed in China

Contents

Series Editors' Preface

The series is designed to fill a niche between publications about universities and colleges that focus exclusively on the practical concerns of university teachers, managers or policy makers and those which are written with an academic, research-based audience in mind that provide detailed evidence, argument and conclusions. The books in this series are intended to build upon evidence and conceptual frameworks in discussing issues which are of direct interest to those concerned with universities. The issues in the series will cover a broad range, from the activities of teachers and students to wider developments in policy at local, national and international levels.

The current pressures on academic and administrative staff, and university managers, mean that only rarely can they justify the time needed to read lengthy descriptions of research findings. The aim, therefore, is to produce compact, readable books that in many parts provide a synthesis and overview of the often seemingly disparate issues.

Some of the books, such as the first in the series – *The University in the Global Age* – are deliberatively broad in focus and conceptualisation, looking at the system as a whole from an international perspective, and are a collection of integrated chapters, written by specialist authors. In other books, such as *Research and Teaching: Beyond the Divide,* the author looks within universities at a specific issue to examine what constitutes 'best practice' through a lens of available theory and research evidence.

Underpinning arguments, where appropriate, with research-based conceptual analysis makes the books more convincing to an academic audience, while the link to 'good practice and policy' avoids the remoteness that comes from an over-abstract approach. The series will thus appeal not just to those working within higher education, but also to a wider audience interested in knowing more about an organisation that is attracting increasing government and media attention.

NOEL ENTWISTLE
ROGER KING

Acknowledgements

Thanks are due to Chrissie Boughey, who generously lent me her beach house on the east coast of South Africa, where I started this book, and to Chris Winberg, who, in serendipitous symmetry, lent me her beach house on the west coast of the same country, where I (almost) finished it. Sue Myburgh and Chris know that I will never be able to look at a pilchard again without smiling. My many friends in South Africa always made my stays there a pleasure: I can never fully repay their generous hospitality, though I will try my best. Thanks particularly to Sue Mathieson for facilitating some of the work there. Thanks too to those readers who commented on early drafts of the book or parts of it, in particular Paul Ashwin, Joelle Fanghanel, Ian McNay, and Terry Wareham as well as anonymous reviewers. Thanks go also to the many people who made suggestions for reading, or gave me critical comments when I talked about the topic of this book in public (which, some would say, I have done all too often!). My son Oliver helped me with the citations and references, so thanks to you Olly. Finally, I need to thank all those people who over the years have participated in my research projects, giving time to something which had no immediate benefit to them. Faults that remain in the book are, as they say, all mine.

Introduction

This book began to take the form it did during a visit to South Africa. I had gone there on a research visit to a university which was undergoing a merger of several previously separate, and very different, institutions. I was not interested in the merger itself but in what the forced interactions between different departments in the same discipline might show about the nature of local cultures within departments. I reasoned that I would be able to see cultural characteristics more clearly in a (to me) novel environment. I also hoped that these forced interactions would make their own particular cultural characteristics more apparent to the local academics themselves. South Africa itself seemed an ideal environment for higher education research. That country, as Johnson (2006) notes, often seems like a vast social science experiment, 'a theatre in which much of the rest of the world finds echoes of its own struggles' (p. vii). Issues of power, ethnicity, and structured disadvantage are still found in an exaggerated form there and so are more obvious to the outsider.

In terms of theory, my thinking was much influenced by the work of Lave and Wenger (1991). I was looking for different *communities of practice*, as they describe them, interacting with each other. What I found surprised and puzzled me. The problem was summed up by one head of department who said, 'there are more factions than people in my department'. Where was the 'community of practice' here, then? What was being revealed largely centred around diversity and conflict, not 'legitimate peripheral participation': gentle induction into a shared set of understandings and practices. And as I reflected on my previous research in universities in the United Kingdom it seemed that the same thing often applied there too: diversity and conflict alongside consensus and community. The notion of cultures within academic departments clearly merited sustained attention.

What the book addresses is change in higher education. It focuses on teaching and learning rather than, for example, research. But it is predicated on the idea that successful changes must address issues at the 'coal face' of higher education: workgroups inside academic departments. And so if leaders and change agents want to 'do' change better they need, among other things, a nuanced understanding and a realistic analytical model at that level. That model needs to be a social one, which takes into account the social practices and the construction of reality as well as the playing out of socially given features there. Strangely, though, academic writing about sociologically oriented approaches to knowledge, knowing, and learning rarely focus themselves on formal educational environments. The sociology of learning and knowing has been applied instead to studies of navigational environments aboard ships (Hutchins, 1995a), decision-making in aircraft cockpits (Hutchins, 1995b), decisions to launch space shuttles (Vaughan, 1996), and so on. Even where education is the focus, rather strange environments are chosen: apprenticeships in the tailoring trade; the manufacturing of pots; and blacksmithing or Mexican midwifery (for example in Lave and Wenger, 1991). The lens used to examine educational practices has been predominantly a psychological, not a sociological one, focussing on the individual not people in interaction with each other and their environment.

I am not sure why this is the case. However, it is fairly clear that it is now time to develop and apply some of the insights of social science to the everyday environments in higher education that many of us know. This exercise will both tell us more about higher education and help us to improve it.

Readers will notice that there is little about *students* in these pages. Self-evidently they are intimately involved in the higher education project and it might seem rather strange to have a book about teaching and learning which says little about them. The primary reason for their absence is that this is a book primarily about change, enhancement efforts rather than teaching and learning itself. It is a book about the practices and attitudes of academic staff, and about movement in these. A secondary reason is that including the student dimension would have made this already-large project a completely unwieldy one. It is for others to bring this important dimension to the discussion.

Clearly, in preparing this book I have drawn on a considerable amount of literature. The book also draws on and in a sense encapsulates the ideas derived from a number of research projects I have been involved in over the years. These have been published in books and articles, written alone or collaboratively. These can be found in the References.

A Note about Audience and Voice in this Book

I sought to write parts of this book in a new, different voice (Gilligan, 1982). The reason for this is to avoid as far as possible the obscuring effect that academic discourse can sometimes have. I found this harder than I'd imagined, but my deficiencies in this area are partly compensated for by the use of vignettes, sometimes drawn from unlikely sources, to elaborate or clarify. My aim is to talk to professionals who happen to be specialists in other fields and disciplines and so who need clear, and interesting, messages about their practical interest in enhancing teaching and learning in universities.

Chapter 1 offers an overview of approaches to culture in universities. Chapter 2 explains the general theoretical background which underpins the concept: sociocultural theory. This is a way of conceptualising the social world more generally, in particular the ways in which the material environment, 'reality', and social life interact. Chapter 3 provides a brief overview of the notion of teaching and learning regimes. Chapter 4 elaborates and deconstructs that theoretical framework, giving examples to illustrate the concepts involved. Chapter 5 examines the organisational dimension – looking at the nature of universities as organisations in which teaching and learning regimes sit and how they may enable or restrict changes designed to improve practices and outcomes in relation to teaching and learning. Chapter 6 applies the ideas developed in earlier chapters to the issue of change, particularly change attempts in terms of the enhancement of teaching and learning. Finally, Chapter 7 looks at ways in which practitioners-as-researchers can investigate their own context in order to help enhancement efforts and examines some of the issues raised in this.

1 Understanding Cultures in Higher Education

This chapter explores alternative approaches to understanding cultures. It begins at the organisational ('macro') level and describes some of the common understandings of culture, most of which are addressed at that level. The chapter then goes on to show the ways in which a social practice-based understanding of culture differs from these.

The level of analysis then shifts to the individual ('micro') level to explore the ways in which individual subjectivities intermesh with their social locale: in other words, to explore the ways in which the micro and macro dimensions of culture are related.

A third and final shift in the level of analysis takes the chapter to the meso level, showing how workgroups at the departmental level in universities are particularly significant in the construction and enactment of cultures. Here a specific example of teaching and learning regimes[1] is used to illustrate the importance of culture at this level. This introduces the following chapter, which provides a more detailed overview of this area.

▶ Culture at the organisational level

'Culture' is an extremely slippery word. Like 'discourse', it is much used, and misused, in social science. Gerth and Mills (1970, p. xxii) suggest that it is a 'word for the lazy'. Perhaps this is not surprising given that some approaches to its use have lacked precision. Phenomenological approaches in particular consider cultures to be uniquely created in each social situation and to be in a state of constant flux. Given this they cannot be easily defined or described. As a result 'culture' is usually understood to mean something like 'the way we do things around here' (Geertz, 1983), involving 'webs of significance' spun by men and women in their daily lives which can only be interpreted, not analysed.

While intuitively comprehensible, this approach offers little analytical purchase. And yet social scientists have long recognised the value of a cultural perspective which 'permits coherent interpretations of events that may seem, at first glance, to be atomistic' (Kuh and Whitt, 1988, pp. 2–3). Thus some writers have attempted to develop approaches to culture that are more easily operationalised. Two of these are the 'nomothetic' approach and the 'inductively derived categorising' (IDC) approach to culture.

Categorising approaches to culture in organisations

'Nomothetic' approaches to organisational culture attempt to categorise types of culture in generalised terms, providing a typology in which to slot specific examples. The term 'nomothetic' also implies that universal, general laws can be established. In this case the laws are about the causal relationship between culture and change. Nomothetic approaches provide a theory about the significance of culture for organisations, particularly in terms of their aims, the significant people and sub-groups within them, the nature of interactions there, and so on.

The nomothetic approach is distinct from idiographic ones such as the phenomenological perspective mentioned above. Idiographic approaches see each example as having unique characteristics which cannot be categorised into a universal schema, and consider it impossible to establish universal laws in the area being considered. Thus each organisational culture found in a university is particular to that institution and must be studied on its own terms.

Nomothetic approaches tend to be functionalist in character. That is, they suggest that organisational culture conditions behaviour and, if it is strong and coherent enough, can facilitate united action towards common and agreed goals. Here 'strength' means the degree to which patterns of behaviour, values, and attitudes permeate an organisation with very little deviance from them. In this way a strong, coherent, and shared set of values and behaviour in an organisation can improve its effectiveness. The role of management, in this view, is to use as many levers as possible to foster strong unitary cultures which are oriented to achieving the vision that leaders set out for organisations. This approach is very clearly set out in Peters and Waterman (1982).

The work of Charles Handy (1993), though not original, is probably the best-known example of a nomothetic approach to culture, though many others have followed his lead. Almost all of them – like him – identify 'four' cultural types. The following outline is drawn from Handy's work.

Handy's four cultures

The power culture. A power culture is frequently found in small entrepreneurial organisations. Its structure is best pictured as a web. This culture depends on a central power source, with rays of power and influence spreading out from that central figure. If the centre chooses the right people, who can think in the same way as it thinks, they can be left to get on with the job. There are few rules and procedures, little bureaucracy. Control is exercised by the centre largely through the selection of key individuals and by occasional forays from the centre or summonses to the centre. These cultures, and organisations based on them, are proud and strong. They have the ability to move quickly and can react well to threat or danger. Whether they do move or whether they move in the right direction will, however, depend on the person or persons in the centre. The quality of these individuals is of paramount importance in those organisations and the succession issue is the key to their continued success. Individuals employed in them will prosper and be satisfied to the extent that they are power-orientated, politically minded, risk-taking, and rate security as a minor element in their psychological contract. Resource power is the major power base in this culture with some elements of personal power in the centre.

The role culture.   The role culture is often stereotyped as bureaucracy. The accompanying structure to a role culture can be pictured as a Greek temple. The role organisation rests its strength in its pillars, its functions or specialities. These pillars are strong in their own right; the finance department, the purchasing department, the production facility may be internationally renowned for their efficiency. The work of the pillars, and the interaction between the pillars, is controlled by procedures. They are co-ordinated at the top by a narrow band of senior management, the pediment. It is assumed that this should be the only personal co-ordination needed, for if the separate pillars do their job, as laid down by the rules and procedures, the ultimate result will be as planned. In this culture the role, or job description, is often more important than the individual who fills it. Individuals are selected for satisfactory performance of a role, and the role is usually so described that a range of individuals could fill it. Performance over and above the role prescription is not required, and indeed can be disruptive at times. Position power is the major power source in this culture, personal power is frowned upon and expert power tolerated only in its proper place. Rules and procedures are the major methods of influence.

The task culture.   The task culture is job- or project-orientated. Its accompanying structure can be best represented as a net, with some of the strands of the net thicker and stronger than the others. Much of the power and influence lies at the interstices of the net, at the knots. The so-called 'matrix organisation' is one structural form of the task culture.

The culture seeks to bring together the appropriate resources, the right people at the right level of the organisation, and to let them get on with it. Influence is based more on expert power than on position or personal power, although these sources have their effect. Influence is also more widely dispersed than in other cultures, and each individual tends to think she has more of it. It is a team culture, where the outcome, the result, the product, of the team's work tends to be the common enemy obliterating individual objectives and most status and style differences. The task culture utilises the unifying power of the group to improve efficiency and to identify the individual with the objective of the organisation. This culture is extremely adaptable. Groups, project teams, or task forces are formed for a specific purpose and can be reformed, abandoned, or continued. The net organisation works quickly since each group ideally contains within it all the decision-making powers required. Individuals find in this culture a high degree of control over their work, judgement by results, and easy working relationships within the group with mutual respect based upon capacity rather than age or status.

The person culture. In this culture the individual is the central point. If there is a structure or an organisation it exists only to serve and assist the individuals within it. If a group of individuals decide that it is in their own interests to band together in order for the better to follow their own bents, to do their own thing, and that an office, a space, some equipment, or even clerical and secretarial assistance would help, then the resulting organisation would have a person culture. It would exist only for the people in it without any super-ordinate objective. Barristers' chambers, architects' partnerships, hippy communes, social groups, families, and some small consultancy firms often have this 'person' orientation. Its structure is as minimal as possible, a 'cluster' is the best word for it, or perhaps a 'galaxy of individual stars'. Clearly, not many organisations can exist with this sort of culture, since organisations tend to have objectives over and above the collective objectives of those who comprise them. Furthermore, control mechanisms, or even management hierarchies, are impossible in these cultures except by mutual consent. The psychological contract states that the organisation is subordinate to the individual and depends on the individual for its existence. The individual can leave the organisation but the organisation seldom has the power to evict the individual.

Berquist's four cultures

The depictions above are clearly drawn in such a way as to apply to any category of organisation. Berquist's work (1992) applies the nomothetic approach to the study of universities in particular. The categories he discerns are the 'collegial', 'managerial', 'negotiating', and 'developmental' cultural types in the higher education system. They are briefly described as follows

Collegial culture. Universities characterised by the collegial culture are centred around the disciplines represented by the academic staff of the institution. Their collaborative work is the key to this cultural form. Research and scholarship are highly valued and there is general agreement that the institution's primary role is the generation, interpretation, and dissemination of knowledge. Great significance is attached to the development of specific values and qualities of character among the young men and women who are students in collegial universities.

Managerial culture. The managerial culture, by contrast, is one that finds meaning primarily in the organisation. Specific goals and purposes are clearly identified and the extent to which they are achieved is carefully evaluated. Economy and efficiency are highly valued and effectiveness as well as supervisory skills are seen as ensuring that these are achieved. The university's primary role is conceived as the inculcation of specific knowledge, skills, and attitudes in students so that they might become successful and responsible citizens.

Developmental culture. The developmental culture is one that finds meaning primarily in the creation of programmes and activities furthering the personal and professional growth of all members of the collegiate community. This culture stresses the value of personal openness and service to others, as well as systematic institutional research and curricular planning. The institution's primary role is conceived as the encouragement of potential for cognitive, affective, and behavioural maturation among all students, faculty, administrators, and other staff. Developmental cultures are sub-species of collegial cultures rather than being a completely distinct category.

Negotiating culture. Finally, the negotiating culture is one that finds meaning primarily in the establishment of equitable and egalitarian policies and procedures for the distribution of resources and benefits in the institution. Value is placed on confrontation and fair bargaining among constituencies (primarily management and academic staff) with vested interests that are inherently in opposition. The university's primary role is conceived as either the undesirable promulgation of existing (and often repressive) social attitudes and structures or the establishment of new and more liberating social attitudes and structures.

McNay's four cultures

McNay (1995) takes a similar view of the four cultures of the academy to Berquist's. Here the four are Collegium, Bureaucracy, Corporation, and Enterprise. They are set out on a matrix as shown in Figure 1.1:

So, Collegium involves a considerable amount of freedom for academics and to some extent for students, while within Bureaucracy regulation becomes important. In the Corporation the executive asserts authority, while in Enterprise professional service to the client dominates behaviour: the desire to 'delight'. All four coexist within a single university, according to McNay, though the balance is different in each case and shifts over time. As with Handy, the essential issue here is where power and decision-making lies. This is a model which describes 'corporate culture', rather than organisational culture in a broader, more sociological sense. A wider understanding of cultures in organisations takes into account values, attitudes, and practices which extend beyond issues of how decisions are made and where power lies, though it incorporates them.

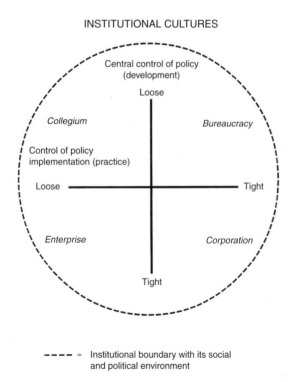

Figure 1.1 McNay's four cultures (McNay, 1995, p. 106 and later elaborated)

An inductive approach to categorising

The approaches just described characterise universities according to four simple categories which are pre-defined and 'imposed' upon them by the person studying them. The IDC approach reverses this, using the characteristics of particular institutions to build a specific conception of culture there. IDC is, therefore, idiographic in character, and is derived from what is observed, not imposed on it. However, this approach seeks to avoid the intangibility of the phenomenological perspective on the one hand and the over-generalising nature of the nomothetic perspective on the other. It attempts to do this by identifying a structure or framework grounded in a study of the individual institution itself. This is then used as a device for subsequent description and analysis. The approach relies upon deriving a set of criteria from the people involved and developing these into an analytic schema.

The work of Bill Tierney (1988) is an example. He conducted a participant observation and interview-based study of Family State College during the academic year 1984–1985. On the basis of this, Tierney offers the following headings for a framework he considers useful for analysing the culture of a higher education institution:

1. *Environment:* How does the organisation define its environment? What is its attitude towards the environment (hostility, friendship)?
2. *Mission:* How is it defined and how is it articulated? Is it used as the basis for decisions? How much agreement is there?
3. *Socialisation:* How do new members become socialised? How is it articulated? What do we need to know to survive/excel in this organisation?
4. *Information:* What constitutes information? Who has it? How is it disseminated?
5. *Strategy:* How are decisions arrived at? Which strategy is used? Who makes decisions? What is the penalty for bad decisions?
6. *Leadership:* What does the organisation expect from its leaders? Who are the leaders? Are there formal and informal leaders?

Tierney uses these general headings to provide a unique but well-ordered description of Family State College which captures its distinctiveness yet could be used as the basis of comparison with other institutions. Tierney acknowledges that in applying the concept of organisational culture in this way he has made no use of its subsets: subculture, anti-culture, or disciplinary culture. This is an important point: the concept of 'culture' used here, like the nomothetic approach, tends to conceive it as unitary and, in a sense, 'official'. Again, the categories employed tend to capture 'corporate culture' – in other words, power relations, decision-making procedures, lines of information flow, corporate strategy, and the rest. It is less successful at capturing relatively organised sets of assumptions, values, and attitudes; unreflective recurrent practices; taken-for-granted knowledge as well as discursive repertoires which permeate (or, rather, *constitute*) everyday life.

An IDC approach – similar to Tierney's and replicating its flaws – is used by Whitcomb and Deshler (1983), who conducted a content analysis of data from 83 interviews with a cross-section of academics and other staff at California State University (CSU). From this they distilled the following clusters of dimensions of that institution's culture which 'emerged' from the data:

a) commitment to the institution
b) unity/community
c) humanistic values
d) academic quality
e) educational opportunity
f) academic freedom
g) ethical values
h) institutional identity

Their description of CSU's culture under these headings was used by the authors to promote awareness of the university's culture, stimulate discussion about it, and improve decision-making there: in other words, for quite 'applied' purposes. Like Tierney's – and possibly as a result of these purposes of the study – the focus of the categories is again upon *corporate* culture.

Similar dimensions to those of Whitcomb and Deshler (1983) could, they argue, be applied to any university, though the cultural description achieved would be unique to the institution. *Cultural audits* attempt to do just this. Management consultants, organisational development (OD) specialists, and others have developed instruments designed to capture culture for more applied purposes. These are analogous to psychometric inventories designed to map individuals' personalities, abilities, and potential. Thus, for example, the 'ethics and values audit' (EVA) at the University of Central Lancashire used a taxonomy as a lens through which to audit the culture of the institution (Henry *et al.*, 1992). This used a multi-method research design incorporating questionnaires, semi-structured interviews, and a values-identification grid based upon

Kelly's repertory grid. The conclusions of EVA were built around ten Themes which profile the ethics and values within the University:

1. An informal supportive staff network emerges. This Theme is based upon values of collaboration and communication. There is evidence of mutual respect and trust inherent within an informal community network.
2. This Theme identifies peer group integrity and indicates some satisfaction for peer group honesty, trust, and mutual respect. . . .
3. A need to value interpersonal relationships recognising openness, honesty, and trust is a Theme that further supports Themes 1 & 2.
4. A Theme that positively values interpersonal relationships based on courtesy is exhibited by colleagues. This is supportive of Theme 3.
5. A Theme emerges that reflects insignificant organisational communication networks and poor information flow. There is some evidence of insufficient collaboration.
6. A Theme of non-participation in important decision-making processes has emerged. There is evidence of a lack of personal autonomy and, by implication, elements of a closed culture.
7. Inappropriate styles of management and practice is a Theme that is supportive of Theme 6. There is some evidence of poor official reporting mechanisms and unsatisfactory ways in which problems and conflicts are resolved. Some dissatisfaction occurs in the ways in which changes and innovations are implemented. There is some abuse of both power and role, when management practices and styles are inappropriate, resulting in the individual feeling undervalued.
8. There is a potentially disruptive and particularly charged working environment which is instrumental in affecting the individual's perception of the 'psychological feel' or climate within the organisation. Once again the individual does not feel valued or respected. This Theme is supportive of Themes 6 & 7.
9. A Theme emerges that clearly indicates dissatisfaction with the provision of staff resources. This refers to teaching, accommodation, provision of staff cover, time for preparation, provision of good library resources, time to develop IGA, and subsequent incentives.
10. A Theme of inappropriate provision for research and advanced study has emerged. Dissatisfaction exists relating to time available to spend with students. Furthermore, there is little time for updating personal expertise. Inherent within this Theme are issues concerning prioritising research and knowledge as educational values, quality of course delivery and the student's experience.

The values identified and considered essential by both staff and management are not always put into practice. ...Some of the 'Themes' identify issues of concern. For example, some contradictions emerge between informal networks and formal processes, Themes 1 and 6.

(Henry *et al.*, 1992, pp. 6–7)

What is notable even in this short extract is the focus on a very limited number of aspects of the ethical and value dimensions of culture: trust, collaboration, information flow, power, and professional respect. Values in higher education (which significantly affect judgements about good and bad, appropriate and inappropriate) are also about, for example, the purposes of higher education, curricular content, teaching methods, priorities in professional life, and so on. These were missed by this audit, yet have important consequences for the life and work of a university. The audit report also generalises about the ethics and values within the *institution* as a whole: the unit of analysis here is the University of Central Lancashire, not any of its organisational sub-units. This focus reveals the assumptions underpinning the study about where the boundaries of culture lie. We will see below that such assumptions may be wrong.

In addition, the Themes drift away from ethics and values to focus also on resources and administrative arrangements. This demonstrates how the different dimensions of culture are interrelated, making it hard to maintain boundaries in discussing them. Any attempt to 'audit' ethics and values will inevitably stray into broader cultural terrain if it is to be of any use. And it is inevitable too that only particular dimensions of culture, even of just its ethical and value components, will be oriented in a way which is structured by the preconceptions of the researchers and what they are looking for. Better, then, if these are made explicit, and so amenable to evaluation by the reader.

The unit of analysis and nomothetic and IDC approaches

With both the nomothetic and the IDC approaches to understanding culture there is no necessity for the unit of analysis to be the institution, though it usually is. A well-known alternative analytical focus is the *discipline*. Here members of disciplinary (as opposed to organisational) communities are depicted as sharing common cultural characteristics. Clearly, for some academics in some university contexts the discipline is more important than for others: Gouldner (1957) sums this up in his distinction between cosmopolitans and locals. The former inhabit the global realm of the discipline while the latter associate more with their institution and are largely restricted to it both physically and in their concerns and activities. The significant level of analysis of culture for cosmopolitans is much higher – at the level of 'invisible college' (Crane, 1972) of their disciplinary community – than it is for locals.

Becher's (1989) and Becher and Trowler's (2001) work in this area uses a broad nomothetic approach and, within that, uses empirical data to draw out categories evident on the ground which delineate differences between the academic tribes' cultural practices. They use the polarities of hard/soft and pure/applied knowledge characteristics as a matrix within which to slot the disciplinary territories. Associated cultural attributes are linked to the polarities urban/rural (mapping the breadth and extent of interactions between academics) and convergent/divergent (having or not having uniformity of standards, procedures, agreement on appropriate topics of study). The knowledge characteristics of disciplines are, they argue, influential in shaping culture so that 'hard/pure' disciplines such as physics tend to have cultural characteristics associated with the urban/convergent category: a strong sense of community may be found in that discipline despite its numerous specialisms. Sociology, by contrast (soft, pure), is 'fissiparous and fragmented'; that is, it displays cultural characteristics associated with the rural/divergent cultural category. Disciplinary allegiances are reflected in the everyday life of academics, in the pictures and objects they choose for their offices, in their conversation, in the metaphors and other forms of language they use, and perhaps even in their leisure activities (Becher, 1989, p. 106).

However, Becher and Trowler (2001, p. 39) are careful to point out that

> To allocate disciplines to domains in the apparently straightforward way that Biglan (1973a, b) and Kolb (1981) have done – alongside the exponents of other taxonomic systems – may be acceptable at a broad general level of analysis, but could prove seriously misleading when subjected to closer and more detailed examination.

As the level of analysis moves from an aerial view to one closer to the ground it is clear that such broad generalisations begin to lose their coherence; the picture becomes far more complex. Thus other categories of difference acquire significance and the boundaries between them increasingly dissolve. Factors such as institutional context of departments, the gender, ethnicity, and background of particular academics, the policy and resource environment play their part in shaping academic cultures differently in different sites. New characteristics evolve, some old ones die away, and so different cultural characteristics are found within the same discipline or even sub-discipline in different institutional locations. The walls of the boxes into which cultural types are slotted become fuzzy and begin to fade.

Whatever the unit of analysis of culture, then, be it the institution, the discipline, or some other unit, diversity and dynamism characterise culture rather than stasis and homogeneity. Recognition of this phenomenon leads us to the next way of understanding cultures: the multiple cultural configuration (MCC) approach.

▶ The multiple cultures in organisations

The MCC perspective on cultures in universities adopts a more nuanced and dynamic approach than those above. It sees cultures in institutions as open, natural systems which are intimately linked to broader cultural contexts. Additionally, it sees cultures as inherently dynamic and interactive.

> [This approach] assumes that organisations can be understood as shaping local versions of broader societal and locally developed cultural manifestations in a multitude of ways. Organisational cultures are then understandable not as unitary wholes or as stable sets of subcultures but as mixtures of cultural manifestations of different levels and kinds. People are connected to different degrees with organisation, suborganisational unit, profession, gender, class, ethnic group, nation, etc; cultures overlap in an organisational setting and are rarely manifested in a 'pure' form. ... It is especially important to keep in mind cultural traffic – that organisations are not cultural islands but are affected by the societal culture. ... [C]ultural configurations vary according to the issue and the ideology in question. The idea of multi cultural configurations takes ambiguity seriously without placing it at the centre of the analysis, and opens up the possibility of 'explaining' much uncertainty, confusion and contradiction.
>
> (Alvesson, 1993, p. 118)

So for Alvesson (2002, pp. 186–187) the kinds of approaches to culture discussed above are guilty of what he calls 'deadly sins' (and, of course, he identifies seven). The most significant of these are treating culture as an 'it', as thing-like, rather than nuanced, dynamic, and protean; treating culture in terms of a few essential traits, giving a too-strongly ordered and superficial picture; and seeing culture as singular rather than multiple, partly as a result of confusion between formal, legal boundaries and cultural ones. He also points out that a *shared* culture is often regarded as a cure-all and a road to effectiveness and efficiency, the functionalist view discussed above. Alvesson acknowledges that the word 'culture' is often used to encompass *everything*, depriving it of meaning. By contrast, the word is also sometimes used in a way that suggests it can be 'captured' and described. Actually such descriptions usually capture only the manifestations of culture, not cultural systems themselves. Thus particular management practices, for example, are often merely indexical of culture, not first-order aspects of organisational culture in themselves.

From an MCC perspective then

- Organisational cultures are *open* (for example, to 'Great Culture' (see p. 23), ethnic and gender-based cultures, student culture, or managerialism). Universities have numerous cultures in operation simultaneously and are open to and affected by the cultural contexts in which they operate.
- There are multiple cultures in a single institution.
- Organisational cultures are dynamic – cultural traffic flows into and through the organisation, washing through new practices, values, attitudes, and discourses.
- Cultural eddies and flows swirl around different issues in different ways.
- Cultures within organisations occupy different 'stages': front-of-stage (the public arena), back-stage (where deals are done), and under-the-stage (where gossip is purveyed). Models of organisational culture which fail to take this into account, perhaps accepting the front-of-stage articulation as 'the' culture, miss much that is important in understanding the cultural life of an institution.
- Cultures are both *enacted* and *constructed*; that is, an organisation's members learn and begin to play out the predominant norms, values, and attitudes in their sector of the organisation (cultural enactment through socialisation). But at the same time they have the power to question, subvert, and change them (cultural construction).
- Organisations are, consequently, *not* 'birth marked' (Grieco, 1988), that is stamped with a particular personality from inception. Neither are they forever shaped by organisational sagas and the personalities of powerful founders, as some American literature on university cultures would have it (for example, Clark, 1972).

The MCC perspective on cultures offers a much more nuanced approach to understanding them, and one which often strikes a chord with people who work in universities. They can usually see how this description applies much more fully than, for example, the nomothetic approach of

Berquist. Yet the cost of the sophistication of the model lies in the difficulties in applying it: studying cultures in universities becomes a rather more difficult and time-consuming affair.

▶ Conclusion – why does it matter?

It is important to be clear about how the organisational cultural context is being conceptualised because the nature of the model used affects approaches to change. Introducing an innovation into a context seen as having a relatively homogenous culture (for example, an entrepreneurial one) or a relatively simple mix of two or three cultural types, with one dominant, appears to be a relatively simple matter. Appropriate questions would be the following: 'where does power lie (and how can it be mobilised)?'; 'how do the aims of this organisation relate to this innovation?'; 'how might the cultural pattern be shifted to be more in line with this innovation?' The appropriate level of analysis in this case would be at the whole-organisation, and a single change can be planned across the whole organisation.

However, adopting a cultural model more like Alvesson's, the MCC approach, shifts the level of analysis down to organisational sub-units. It suggests that what might work in one part of the organisation may not work, or even find acceptance, in another. It also indicates that a 'market gardening' rather than an agribusiness approach to innovation might be the better one; policy-making and innovation pitched at the local level, not across the organisation as a whole.

These distinctions are important. The main reason why Kezar and Eckel's (2002) attempt to match good approaches to innovation with different organisational cultural types is so unsatisfactory is that they start with an inappropriate model of organisational culture. Quoting other authors, they define culture as

> the deeply embedded patterns of organizational behavior and the shared values, assumptions, beliefs, or ideologies that members have about their organization or its work.
>
> (Peterson and Spencer, 1991, p. 142, quoted in
> Kezar and Eckel, p. 438)

But of course such a definition is imbued with a number of assumptions which almost certainly do not hold true, thus invalidating the whole attempt to match successful change strategies to cultural characteristics, defined in this way. To paraphrase a well-used saying about this, 'all models are wrong, but some are a good deal more useful than others'.

So, this book assumes cultures in universities to be multiple, generated and sustained at the level of the workgroup within departments: the organisational sub-units that Alvesson's model highlights. Therefore, in addressing the issue of culture it is necessary to go down to this level. But first I want to elaborate a set of theoretical tools that help in looking at the social world at this level and beyond it, summarised under the general heading of 'Sociocultural Theory'.

2 A Sociocultural Understanding of Teaching, Learning, and Assessment

The proper study of interaction is not the individual and his [or her] psychology, but rather the syntactical relations among acts of different people mutually present to one another ... Not, then, [wo]men and their moments. Rather, moments and their [wo]men.

(Goffman, 1967, p. 3)

They travel in disguise and often under alias – attitudes, values, judgements, axioms, opinions, ideology, perceptions, conceptions, conceptual systems, preconceptions, dispositions, implicit theories, personal theories, internal mental processes, action strategies, rules of practice, practical perspectives, repertories of understanding, and social strategy, to name but a few that can be found in the literature.

(Pajares, 1992, cited in Kane et al., 2002, p. 181)

Most Americans have been to school and know what a 'real school' is like. Congruence with that cultural template has helped maintain the legitimacy of the institution ... But when schooling departed too much from the consensual model of a 'real school', failed to match the grammar of schooling, trouble often ensued. ... For their part, teachers also have had an investment in the familiar institutional practices of the school. They learned these as students, and as they moved to the other side of the desk, they often took traditional patterns of organization for granted as just the way things were. ... Both general beliefs in the broader culture about what a 'real school' was and the hold of standard operating procedures on staff and students put a brake on innovators who sought basic changes in classroom instruction.

(Tyack and Cuban, 1995, pp. 9–10)

▶ Sociocultural theory

Sociocultural theory can be summarised in terms of a number of propositions. The first is that as workgroups engage in common projects over the medium to long term they develop sets of ways of behaving (recurrent practices), ways of understanding their world (taken-for-granted knowledge), and ideas about what is good and bad (values). In short, they are involved in the social construction of reality, at least in the areas of common engagement that they have. At the root of this is the process of weaving webs of meaning in, around, and through 'reality'. Meaning is 'situated in specific social and cultural practices and is continually transformed in those practices' (Gee, 1999, p. 63). Fences are built which categorise and separate 'this' from 'that' (Bowker and Star, 1999), especially 'us' from 'them', and these fences are carefully maintained. Meanwhile, deep wells of significance are dug into signs and symbols. Those wells of significance are further deepened and strengthened in the drawing from them, as they are mobilised into use. Conflicts and divisions often exist, but these are partly the product of social construction too.

The second proposition states that people's interaction with objects (artefacts, tools, technologies, devices) is socially mediated: the objects themselves may influence the nature of social reality in significant ways, while their use is at the same time socially conditioned. Artefacts both 'configure' activity while simultaneously being imbued with particular meaning and significance by their users. This shapes their use.

A third proposition is that workgroups develop sets of discursive repertoires, which both express social realities and operate to constrain and delimit them: the production of text in discourse and the construction of reality work side by side, mirroring the operation of structure and agency in social interaction.

According to the fourth proposition, in terms of the project they are mutually engaged on, workgroups develop unique ways of using the tools available to them and a context-specific understanding of aspects of their project. They produce the components of a definitive, and unique, mental model as they assemble, construct, and negotiate knowledge and meaning and apply it to their task. Because of this socially constructive process it is necessary to go beyond the individual level of analysis and to study, as Goffman recommends (1967, p. 3), the relational actions of people in groups.

The fifth proposition states that individual identities, or subjectivities, are similarly mediated and conditioned by social context. Our constructions of 'self' are partly the product of the social contexts and social relations within the institutions we inhabit.

The sixth proposition is that historical background, or at least narratives about the past constructed by participants, has very significant influences on social life in the present.

As a result of this series of ideas it is clear that social context is a very significant dimension of values and practices. As a result, any attempt to generalise across social contexts is fraught with danger. What works in one place may not work in another. What is 'true' in one place may not be the case in another. As one head of department (HoD) quoted in Knight and Trowler (2001) said,

> At one university I seemed to have the Midas touch...That university was much more informal than the one I presently work in and creativity in administration was admired and encouraged. There were very few of the structures there are here...Since I came here I find creative administration is inhibited by structure. ...You could say the atmosphere is much more business-like here...I am not as good at leadership here, partly I think because I am not the world's most meticulous administrator

Eraut comments that

> to understand any situation involving several people we need to adopt two complementary perspectives. One should focus on the situation itself – its antecedents, wider context and ongoing interaction with its environment – and the transactions of its participants throughout the period of enquiry. The other should focus on the contribution of the situation to the learning careers of individual participants, the learning acquired during their 'visit'. From a situational perspective knowledge is already present in established activities and cultural norms and imported through the contributions of new participants. From an individual perspective, some of their prior knowledge is resituated in the new setting and integrated with other knowledge acquired through participation. According to the magnitude of the impact of the 'visit', their knowledge can be described as having been expanded modified or even transformed.
>
> (Eraut, 2000, pp. 131–132)

▶ Sociocultural and psychological approaches: The need for rebalancing

Much of the study of teaching and learning in higher education has been conducted from the perspective of the discipline of psychology. While there is nothing wrong with this, the dominance of that discipline has led in some cases to the problems associated with psycholog*ism* – adopting the individual person as the significant level of analysis and, potentially at least, conceiving that person as existing in a cultural, historical, institutional, and micro-social vacuum. This is not a new point. John Dewey argued in his 1901 presidential address to the American Psychological Association that the discipline was analytically handicapped by its exclusive focus on the individual. This becomes a problem when ideas based only on the individual, or the dyad, are taken up and used in educational practice. The relationship between the individual and their context becomes hidden so that both learners and educators are conceptualised in a disembodied way. Obscuring the impact of institutional context, which so often has important influences on values and practices, is particularly unhelpful.

The significance of context tends to be absent in the residual elements of ideas about teaching and learning that remain when theory and research are translated into daily practice. This is illustrated in the example of the influential 'approaches to learning' tradition in higher education, originally developed in Gothenburg, focused on differing ways in which students go about the task of learning. Students' intentions were significant, but their approaches to learning were also conditioned by what was being learned and the context of learning, particularly the way teaching and assessment were conducted (see Entwistle, 2007, for an overview of this tradition). So students adopted a deep (understanding) or surface (memorising) approach, the deep approach being preferable. Other approaches were also identified in this research. A key point was that the approach to learning was not an inherent characteristic of the student but could be evoked by curricular design. Unfortunately, the significance of context, in this sense, is often lost, as an instructional video about this issue unwittingly demonstrates:

http://video.google.com/videoplay?docid=-5629273206953884671.

In the application of such ideas it is easy to lose sight of context because the focus is on the range of conceptions and approaches available to the *individual*. The affective side of practice can be lost sight of too, because the focus is on cognition. Ashwin (2008) comments as follows:

In examining this *approaches to learning* research in terms of structure and agency, there are two major problems with the explanations that are offered. First, because this research approach is focused on students' and educators' *perceptions* of teaching and learning environments, they are firmly rooted in considerations of agency. Anything that operates outside of these perceptions is bracketed outside of explanations offered. ...Second, 'approaches to learning' research is only focused on academics and students *as* educators and learners. It is only those aspects of teaching and learning situations that are directly related to teaching and learning that are considered relevant within these research studies. As a result this tradition focuses on 'disembodied' learners and teachers and tends to underplay the importance of their identities and power relations in teaching and learning interactions. This means that academics, students, and their institutional contexts cease to have a history: the explanatory framework is ahistorical. Thus it is unsurprising that, despite the huge changes that have taken place in, for example, the composition of the student body, student: staff ratios, and the number and types of universities since the learning approach was first developed in the 1970s, its basic explanation of TLA (teaching, learning and assessment) interactions has remained largely unchanged.

▶ A focus on the workgroup

What is in need of rebalancing here is an understanding of teaching and learning in their social contexts, of the figure situated in its ground. In particular, the missing level of analysis is the meso level – the point of social interaction by small groups such as those existing in the classroom, in the university department, in the curriculum-planning team, or in a hundred other task-based teams within the higher educational system.

Workgroups within departments are the most significant aspect of social life for the individuals involved: when people go to work at their university they go to their department. They think about their immediate colleagues and the events which they recurrently engage in. It is, in short, the most salient dimension of social life for participants.

Yet this level of analysis in thinking about organisational life is often missing, not only in the study of higher education (as Tight's study, discussed on pp. 56–7, showed) but also in the study of organisations and management:

> For many years, students of organizations divided their field of studies into two categories – micro and macro. This distinction presumed two levels of analysis. The micro level dealt with individual human beings and, to a somewhat lesser extent, individuals working together in groups. The macro level focused primarily on organizations as a whole, especially their structures, and interactions with an even larger system, i.e. the organization's environment.
>
> (Clegg *et al.*, 1999, p. 5)

If the social world can be understood at the micro level of individual sub-jectivity and/or at the organisational and societal macro level then why should it be important to devote more attention to the meso level?

One answer is that this level of analysis allows us to see the operation of the micro and the macro brought together at the meso level:

> The collective activity system [interacting individuals focused on a task], as unit of analysis, connects the psychological, cultural and institutional perspectives to analysis. The study of activity ceases to be the psy-chology of an individual but instead focuses on the interaction between an individual, systems of artifacts, and other individuals in historically developing institutional settings.
>
> (Miettinen, 1999, p. 174)

However, the focus on meso level is simply a *choice*. Given the com-plexity and interconnectedness of social life the analyst must select both a level of analysis and a particular substantive area on which to focus their study. In doing so they distinguish between *figure* and its *ground* (see p. 56 for a fuller discussion). This is an analytical distinction, not an ontological one. Different choices mean shifting boundaries: a new figure and different ground.

There is no claim here that the meso level is in any sense ontologically superior to other levels of analysis. Macro structures impinge on daily life for individuals and groups in very significant ways. Meanwhile, practices of individuals and groups change the larger structures on an ongoing basis.

In contrast to a psychologistic approach, a focus on the social dimen-sion at the meso level ideally foregrounds social processes in the following ways:

- Rather than taking a snapshot of, for example, lecturers' conceptions of teaching, a focus on local cultures adopts a processual approach which unpacks the dynamic social relations in particular contexts. It should see the teaching and learning situation as ongoing sets of dialogues in a social context, and show how that context conditions teaching and learning practices of different sorts.
- Rather than assuming that the individual 'picks up' knowledge, skills, and attitudes and so can transfer them from place to place, a socio-cultural theory of teaching and learning should problematise 'place' and situate practices within it. In so doing the contingency of knowing and practice is emphasised.

- Rather than taking a snapshot of the educators and learners fixed in time, a sociocultural theory of learning should involve an appreciation of history: of 'presage' broadly conceived, and of the narrativity around that history.
- A social theory of teaching and learning should take into account the affective domain as well as the cognitive, foregrounding the significance of emotional responses in the development of meaning and of knowing.
- A social theory of teaching and learning should conceptualise individuals as discursively and actually moving between alternative positions in relation to teaching and learning, ones which are contextually contingent. This is distinguished from approaches which seek to categorise them into fixed 'types'.

However, this is not to say that a social theory is better than a psychological one; merely that rebalancing towards the social is needed because of the historical dominance of the psychological perspective. Wertsch (1998, p. 9) notes the unhealthy antinomy between individualistic and social conditioning theories of social change:

> It is essential for sociocultural research to formulate its position vis-a-vis this antinomy between individual and society. If it does not, such research is likely to be misunderstood or falsely categorised.

He argues convincingly that the very formulation of issues in either/or alternatives is counterproductive. Rather than having an independent existence, Wertsch sees individualism and social conditioning as hypothetical constructs – conceptual tools which, in sociocultural analysis, are interdependent. Wertsch cites the work of Burke (1969) and others who developed arguments transcending this distinction.

▶ Structure and agency in workgroups

Much of what has been said above indicates that a sociocultural theory is social constructionist in nature: workgroups construct and dispute meaning as they engage together on common projects over time. While they do develop unique meanings and practices, workgroups do not have total control over all aspects of social reality – they are not completely agentic. Social structures limit their room for manoeuvre and influence the workings of the group in important ways. Cultures are *enacted* as well as *constructed* (Tierney, 1987). Here I am using the word 'structure' to mean properties which lend coherence and relative permanence to social practices in different times and locales (Giddens, 1984). These may include cultural characteristics associated with the larger society in which they exist ('Great Culture', as Alvesson, 2002, calls it), gendered aspects of behaviour, professional values, and the oper-ation of power vested in authority. Structures consist of both *rules*, with normative elements and codes of signification, as well as *resources*, which comprise both authoritative and allocative aspects (Giddens, 1984, pp. xxxi, 17).

In terms of teaching and learning, one significant social structural force is the socialisation process that occurs in early schooling. Entwistle *et al.* (2000), citing a number of sources – Korthagen (1993), Pendry (1997), Calderhead (1996), Tillema (1997), and Sugrue (1997) – note that images, metaphors, and beliefs about teaching and learning in schools appear to be established before students begin training as school teach-ers and can be quite resistant to change, while notions of 'good teaching' and emerging identities as teachers are substantially influenced by prior beliefs. Tillema, for example, concluded that teachers generally 'hold on to certain beliefs as being central to their thinking, reasoning and action' (1997, p. 211). Entwistle *et al.* suggest that 'Newly appointed lecturers in higher education can be expected to hold equivalent beliefs and guid-ing metaphors which affect their ways of thinking about teaching, and even established staff continue to be influenced by their initial beliefs and by experiences when they were students' (2000, p. 9). However, they do find that schoolteachers in training are so strongly influenced in their conceptions of 'good teaching' by the teacher education course itself that this can alter their prior conceptions.

This illustrates one sense in which workgroup cultures are 'open' sys-tems: flowing into them with their newly recruited members are sets of preconceptions and assumptions from early life which influence values, attitudes, and practices within the group itself. In addition, departmental interactions (for example, holding a departmental staff meeting) operate in a context which is permeable to influence from external structures such as the sets of recurrent practices pertaining to 'meetings' found in a spe-cific university. Systems of interaction are 'open' in another sense too – open to different dimensions of social life: the economic and the psycho-logical, for example. Social interaction therefore operates in a network of practices.

This means that there are no 'real' boundaries between different social groups. But there are very significant boundaries in people's minds. Iden-tity – both collective and individual – is largely defined in terms of what one is *not* as well what one *is*, on thinking done in terms of categories and distinctions. While these may have limited validity in fact, they are intensely significant subjectively.

So social interactions associated with the specific event – say the departmental meeting – are conditioned by the history and subjectivities of the individuals involved, by the larger organisational context, and by aspects of broader cultures associated with, for example, differences of gender and ethnicity pertinent to the event.

Workgroups also tend to ossify over time so that local structural factors cast their shadow over more' agentic characteristics. These are 'social practices' which Chouliaraki and Fairclough define as 'habitualised ways, tied to particular times and places, in which people apply resources (material or symbolic) to act together in the world' (1999, p. 21).

For Berger and Luckmann (1967) this process is 'institutionalisation', the gradual hardening of behaviour into taken-for-granted patterns of recurrent behaviour enacted in future instances of those same circumstances. Recurrent behaviours develop which are usually so normalised for participants that they are invisible: the participants have sets of expectations, and conventions of appropriate behaviour and of the subjectivities involved in events which structure what happens and lend professional episodes a certain degree of regularity. There are unreflective typifications involved, which Lave and Wenger (1991) call 'reification'. At the same time, however, there are contrasting sets of behaviours within the same social locale, with the same participants acting very differently from each other in what are essentially the same social situations. In other locales with different participants the practices which constitute events with the same names (a departmental staff meeting, an undergraduate seminar, and so on) may be fundamentally different, though equally normalised for those involved.

So, through a unique mix of both agentic and structural factors each workgroup will have aspects of social reality unique to it, created through social interaction over the longer term. These will impinge in important ways on any proposed changes to practices, which will be interpreted and implemented in ways mediated by pre-existing local cultures. Again, outcomes will be relatively unpredictable to anyone not familiar with the specifics of local cultures, as will the ways in which those proposed changes will be received and interpreted by workgroups on the ground.

This interaction between structure and agency, between the forces in social life which impose regularity on our behaviour and our ability to operate freely, is what Giddens calls 'structuration'. People, acting together, are – to sum up – both carriers and creators of webs of meaning.

Agency continues to operate within an environment characterised by such institutionalised social practices because of the dynamic nature of the situation. Practices are challenged by tensions in social interactions, by challenges to the status quo, by external developments, by the inter-action of subjectivities, and by social practices. The significant question is really not 'why do things change?' but 'how do they ever achieve stability in the first place?' The appearance of stability in social life in post-industrialism is deceptive: the situation is a homeostatic one: stability maintained dynamically.

> ## Vignette: Structure and agency, macro trends and ground level responses: Teaching and learning regimes in law schools[2] (adapted from Cownie, 2004)

Theories of teaching and learning, and tacit assumptions and conventions of appropriateness, can change over time nationally or even globally. In the United Kingdom, the teaching of legal skills nationally has moved from the rather conservative outcomes-led model in the 1980s to an increasingly reflective model.

In law the key divisions are between Black Letter law, socio-legal approaches, and critical legal studies, which include feminist approaches and critical race scholarship, for example. Black Letter, or doctrinal, law is concerned with the body of rules and legal skills, more oriented to description and skill acquisition than critical evaluation. Socio-legal studies, by contrast, encompasses a diversity of approaches drawing on other disciplines but generally seeing law and its application in the social context. Critical legal studies, which spread from the United States in the early 1980s, is more radical though aligned in many ways with socio-legal studies. Critical lawyers, though, tend to be hostile to legal rules and draw more on, for example, Marx or feminist scholar-ship and on a range of post-modern theories than on liberal theory. These three approaches are congruent with three educational ideologies identified elsewhere (p. 173): traditionalism (Black Letter law); progres-sivism (socio-legal approaches); and social reconstructionism (critical legal studies).

Snaith's (1990) survey, conducted in 1989, of 24 institutions teach-ing Company Law, 19 universities, and 5 polytechnics (institutions which were designated universities after 1992 in the United Kingdom) showed that at that time the overwhelming pattern of teaching was by lectures and tutorials. Snaith comments that the information on teaching methods demonstrated a rather conservative approach dominating, with lectures and fortnightly tutorials assessed by examination and a small number of textbooks recommended, course content tending to follow the order and substance of those books. Most respondents used examinations (alone) as the summative assessment method, though a quarter used coursework and examination combined. Interestingly, the responses about the objectives of courses suggested a considerable emphasis on Black Letter law, 100% mentioning the development of skills in the use of legal techniques while only 44% mentioned a critical approach to law. However, it may be that this response suggests that these skills were, as Cownie (2004) suggests, seen as a necessary foundation (and therefore ubiquitous) though not in themselves the prime purpose of legal education. Qualitative responses, though, suggested that three perspectives were in evidence in many courses: what Snaith calls 'Black Letter', 'law in context', and 'reconciliation of competing interests', the last analysing the different positions of, for example, shareholders, employees, consumers, and the general public with regard to Company Law. One respondent did refer to a conflict model, indicating a critical legal studies approach.

Ten years later, Cownie conducted interviews with 54 legal academics in law schools in England between 2001 and 2002 (Cownie, 2004, p. 29). She writes,

> In terms of the culture of the discipline, the results of my interviews gave weight to the argument . . . . that law is a discipline in transition, coming from a tradition which was focused exclusively on legal rules, in which any attempt to introduce evidence about the social consequences or political origins of law was regarded as 'irrelevant', to a situation in which a knowledge of traditional doctrinal techniques of analysis is merely the starting point for an exploration of legal phenomena, using a variety of different techniques drawn from an increasingly wide range of disciplines.
>
> (Cownie, 2004, p. 65)

Cownie reports that there was a noticeable level of consensus among legal academics that their principal aim was to teach students to think for themselves. 'The basics' needed to be taught – ensuring that students understand the legal materials they have to deal with – but beyond that academics were concerned to get students to think. None of Cownie's respondents mentioned preparing students for entry to the legal profession as one of their educational aims, and nobody mentioned teaching vocational skills. She reports that academic lawyers find it frustrating when their subject is characterised as 'vocational', and for them the demarcation between academic law and legal practice is well defined.

Things changed markedly then between Snaith and Cownie's surveys, in terms of the aims and content of legal education, a change put into broader historical perspective by Bradney (1992), whose history of university law schools in Britain suggests there has been a process of 'academic drift' (Pratt and Burgess, 1974) with the gradual loss of connections with the practising legal profession.

However, there is still a diversity of approaches to be found within law schools according to Cownie. Given that practices are at least loosely coupled to philosophies, values, beliefs about education, and the rest, this means that teaching practices which reflect the different assumptions underpinning them are adopted. Cownie writes,

The existence of these fundamentally different approaches to law clearly brings with it the possibility of conflict between legal academics, of a kind which is not unknown in law schools. The conflicts resulting from the introduction of the critical legal studies movement into US law schools have been well documented... [however] the conflict of the extreme kind experienced [there] appeared to be unknown among the English legal academics I interviewed. In most cases, respondents specifically described the culture of their department as 'pluralistic'; the norm was that different views were respected. Occasionally, however, tensions rose to the surface, and divisions, while not leading to schism, could be quite great. The attempted marginalisation of socio-legal scholars was certainly an issue in one of the law schools I visited. [One respondent said]:

'I think there is an element in the department that probably doesn't really have much time, or even respect, for that kind of teaching, which is reflected in their attitude. Not just feminism, but socio-legal in general. Hence the discussion about 'this wing of the department and that wing of the department'. It's almost as if people interested in that sort of activity have been hived off and can occupy their own little corridor, or whatever, rather than belonging to the department. Some lacklustre people regard socio-legal is as marginal really.

I think perhaps it's a certain arrogant attitude [on the part of these Black letter people], reflective of their own education, bringing their own perception of what should be regarded as hard law and what should be regarded as easy law. I think some people take the view that hard law is being immersed in the minutiae of the companies act or something like that, so they see socio-legal as easy.'

(Cownie, 2004, p. 59)

Another respondent commented that

> [My approach is] Black Letter. But I think it's essential that a law school of our size should be able to embrace the whole spectrum. We each have a different role to fulfil. There has to be tolerance. I'm a bit suspicious of socio-legal courses, but having made that previous comment, and bearing in mind that lots of students will do things other than being lawyers, we've got to be academically tolerant.
>
> (Cownie, 2004, p. 60)

Most of Cownie's respondents regarded their departments as containing a variety of outlooks. Feminism had become quite commonplace, though around 50% of legal academics interviewed reacted negatively to this and there was some student resistance reported too. This pluralism is reflected in the textbooks which have begun to take a more critical approach than traditional textbooks have done.

However, liberal pluralism, while perhaps desirable, is not evident in every context. Austin (1998) tells the vivid story of the shift from a consensual approach to law in the United States in the early 1970s (such that law students carried on studying while Revolution was breaking out on campuses throughout America) to a situation of open conflict in law schools. Likewise, Tushnet (1990) notes that in the United States 'many liberal academics do not find critical legal studies...easy to live with' (p. 1543), partly because they represent a 'disruptive political presence'.

In some places in the United States there were bitter battles in university departments around the nature of law. Tushnet (1990) recounts the situation at the Yale Law School in the late 1960s and early 1970s in a way which demonstrates the porosity of local cultures:

> The faculty of the law school meanwhile had undergone a significant expansion at the junior level, and the younger faculty became tainted by the mere presence of students who were only a bit younger. In addition, though few of the junior faculty had radical politics, they were all substantially more sympathetic to the claims being made by students than were many of the senior faculty. The senior faculty took on the air of a beleaguered garrison, defending the ramparts at all costs against the assaults of the barbarians. Those who suggested even in the mildest way that the students might be on to something were politically unreliable. Under the circumstances, any disagreement threatened the institutional stability to which many of the senior faculty were dedicated.
>
> (Tushnet, 1990, p. 1531)

Austin offers a short introduction to critical legal studies by way of a vignette (Austin, 1998, pp. 83–84).

> When he left to visit a southern law school, Fino was ensconced in the accepted career groove. He published several long and dense articles with a high footnote density ratio while becoming an irritating bore at faculty meetings. Although the students did not have a clue about what he said in class, they appreciated his fashion – an ascot, crimson blazer with Harvard crest, and a cane.
>
> What a difference a year can make. The students were the first to pick it up: 'He was always out to lunch, but now it is pure countertalk; everything involves "indeterminacy", "oppression", and "opposition". He says that he deconstructs the cases, whatever that means. I liked him better when he was just your typical faculty phoney.'
>
> We got it at the first full faculty meeting when Fino unloaded a new vocabulary of praxis, deification, intersubjective zap, purposinist, altruism – all in a brief 30 minute spirited attack on 'Liberal hegemony'. From then on, everything was a 'mask'. Fino said:.... 'The law is a major vehicle for the maintenance of existing social and power relations.' .... 'Legal reasoning is an inherently repressive form of interpretive thought that limits our comprehension of the social world and its possibilities.'
>
> Then Fino started complaining to any unfortunate soul he could corner about being 'alone'. If I want to discuss a new mask that I have uncovered, I have to call... someone at Miami.
>
> Then, with no warning, the show stopped. Fino dropped the mask talk and went on to Buddhism.

▶ Commentary

This vignette demonstrates issues to do with subjectivity, discourse, as well as perhaps power, conventions of appropriateness, and the tensions and conflicts within cultural contexts. What is also noticeable here is the role of law as a discipline. Clearly the nature of academic law is imposing some structural constraints on what lawyers do. However, academics are making choices from a range of ideological resources and in a sense subscribing to a particular narrative about what academic law actually is. What is happening represents both structure and agency in operation. Fino, for example, has made a choice and changed his discourse and practices completely. However, he did not invent either his old or his new persona from scratch: discursive and other structural resources were already in place and Fino simply switched between them. As people move between different ideological positions, what they teach and how they teach will alter too because what they are trying to achieve is different. Someone shifting towards critical legal studies, and a social reconstructionist position, will not be interested in educating 'legal barbarians' who know very little beyond the law itself. Rather, there will tend to be an emphasis on developing the critical faculties of the person through engagement with broader issues.

► Relevant dimensions of sociocultural theory

The issue of intersubjectivity

I noted above that a theme in some strands of sociocultural theory is the development of discourse communities that are characterised by intersubjectivity, that is by mutually understood ways of interpreting and producing text and by common sets of understandings. Wenger (1998, pp. 125–126) suggests that membership of a community of practice involves the

> rapid flow of information ... absence of introductory preambles as if conversations and interactions were merely the continuation of an ongoing process ... knowing what others know ... local lore, shared stories ... jargon and shortcuts to communication [and] ... shared discourse.

Members of these 'interpretive communities' understand each other well and will tend to interpret texts in the same way. I give an example of such a thing happening on pp. 86–87. It is dangerous, however, to assume that such a situation is the norm. As Rommetveit says,

> The basic problem of human intersubjectivity becomes ... a question concerning in what sense and under what conditions two persons who engage in a dialogue can transcend their different private worlds. And the linguistic basis for this enterprise, I shall argue, is not a fixed repertory of shared 'literal' meanings but very general and partially negotiated drafts of contracts concerning categorisation and attribution inherent in ordinary language. (1979, p. 7)

In everyday monolingual interaction we too easily assume that intersubjectivity has been achieved (Blum-Kulka, 1997), although this has long been recognised by scholars within linguistics (for example, Dretske, 1981; Smith, 1982) to be a complex matter.

The hybrid Deaf-hearing workgroup studied by Trowler and Turner (2002) surfaced this issue in a particularly stark way. This workgroup consisted of Deaf academics (the capital letter denoting alignment with Deaf culture as well as a characteristic of hearing), non-signing hearing academics, and signing hearing academics. The study showed that 'mutual knowledge', intersubjectivity, is not unproblematically achieved. Face-to-face interaction between Deaf academics and non-signing hearing colleagues is always mediated through an interpreter. The interpreting task is never a mere 're-coding' of a message from a source language into a target language, but requires judgements on the part of the interpreter about the intent of the producer and the frames of reference of the receiver (Wadensjo, 1998; Metzger, 1999; Harrington and Turner, 2000). This is particularly so here because the modalities of the two languages are quite different: one is oral/aural while the other is physical/visual. It is the interpreter's professional responsibility to judge where she must provide a bridge between the incompatible knowledgeabilities of interactants. One of the ways to do this is to pass responsibility back to the producer for making more explicit his/her intended meaning. The regularity with which this happens gives an indication of how readily we are used to assuming, wrongly, that our interlocutor is able to 'read off' intended meaning in an unproblematic way. This procedure foregrounds the limited mutuality of knowledgeability in many situations and problematises assumptions about mutuality of interpretation and understanding.

This should make us reconsider the operation of mutual understanding in monolingual settings too, and acknowledge the limits to the homogeneity of participants' mutual knowledgeabilities. Even in tight 'communities' of practice there is more talking *past* each other than we assume when we imagine, incorrectly, that participants are sending and receiving on the same wavelength.

Tools used by workgroups

Social practices involve more than just social interaction; they involve 'tools' and other resources. Examples in university life include the more obvious tools such as email and telephone systems as well as less obvious ones such as organisational structures. Workgroups utilise tools and resources as they engage in recurrent practices to achieve sets of goals. An undergraduate teaching team use particular textbooks and workbooks as they engage with students; the way these are structured shapes practice in the classroom and to some extent may homogenise it. Yet at the same time contextual characteristics mean that the texts are used in unique ways. Thus an iterative process of influence occurs: social practices undergo change as they utilise the tools, and the context of practice, in turn, influences the specific ways in which tools and other resources are used.

In this perspective tools are not completely distinct from the individual or their social context. Rather, tool use is socially and historically conditioned and at the same time the insertion of tools into a social context changes both that context and the way the tool is used: an interactive process occurs between tools and context. Almost all tools, therefore, are 'cultural tools'. They are almost always 'appropriated' (Bakhtin, 1981) or 'domesticated' – that is, they are subtly altered in use to align better with the context of use. Thus, for example, the texting function of mobile phones was never expected by manufacturers to be a significant part of their appeal yet amongst some social groups it is very significant and new forms of language use and communicative practices have developed, mediated by this tool in unexpected and unpredictable ways. This example also highlights the semiotic dimension of tools: the fact that they acquire codes of signification. Mobile phones are not *just* tools to most people: particular models, styles, and functionality (even if not actually used) carry symbolic meaning. Another example is the use of virtual learning environments (VLEs) in universities. Some universities insist that all courses 'must' have a VLE while others adopt a laissez-faire approach. The nature and extent of their use is monitored to a different extent in different contexts, and their use and significance varies widely.

Like symbols and language itself, tools develop overlays of associations and are responded to in ways which are both cognitive and emotional: they are 'marked' by their users, imprinted by history and context (de Certeau, 1984). Some become privileged, others do not.

Assessment practices provide an example. The proposed introduction of self- and peer-assessment (which are pedagogical tools) into the curriculum design potentially represents a significant social experiment as well as a pedagogical one. Textbooks such as Heywood (2000) miss this significant dimension when they treat peer- and self-assessment by students only in technical terms: the effect they have on the provision of feedback; the development of evaluative skills; the effectiveness of assessment of group work; and questions about the validity and reliability. Yet introducing these assessment tools, if undertaken 'properly' and to any significant extent, will reshape relationships and power relations, changing the climate of the classroom, identities, and patterns of interaction. The 'sage on the stage' may find himself/herself thrust into being 'the guide at the side', and this is not always welcome. So, evidence about the relative accuracy of peer-assessment, or about the extent to which it is successful in students' understanding of assessment standards and criteria (O'Donovan *et al.*, 2004), for example, is only part of the story. Successful implementation will also involve sensitivity to wider issues of power relationships and subjectivities, the deeper symbolic significance of change (Wertsch, 1998, p. 66).

In higher education the use of e-mail has changed the nature of social relations in important ways. Meanwhile, the pre-existing cultural characteristics have conditioned the ways in which that technology has been employed. Different cultural contexts imply different methods of tool use and it is sometimes difficult to predict how new tools will be employed and the impact they will have on practices, relationships, and ways of working.

Tools help set the context for action and in so doing develop, on the one hand, certain 'affordances' (Gibson, 1979; Still and Costall, 1989) and, on the other, limit possibilities. An example is the use of pedagogical tools such as 'buzz groups' (small groups of students given a short period to discuss a topic in the classroom and reach a conclusion about it). Like discursive use, using buzz groups enhances certain possibilities (engagement and discussion with the topic) but closes off others (independent learning about the topic, for example).

The use of particular tools can be contentious and the introduction of new tools may give rise to debates within social groups about whether the possibilities opened are worth those that have been closed. Indeed, there may even be debates about whether the new tools have changed in fundamental ways the practices which they are designed to enhance. The debate over the use of calculators in maths classes and exams is one example (Wertsch, 1998). For some, their introduction means that students are no longer 'really' doing maths at all. Similarly, the introduction of certain pedagogical techniques in universities may mean, for some, that what is happening is not 'really' higher education any more. The following extract from Neil Mackay's electoral address to the Institute for Learning and Teaching (ILT) (subsequently incorporated into the Higher Education Academy) provides an example of this kind of thinking about the use of 'jargon' and 'infant-school' games as new tools in HE:

> The ILT has an important role to play in resisting the creeping infantilisation of students in HE institutions and in encouraging students' own sense of responsibility to learn. ... We must treat each other as intelligent adults, just as we would treat our students... There must be no place... for the use of *jargon*... *or infant-school games*.
>
> (Mackay, 2001, p. 5: emphasis mine)

Thus the use of new tools, or the extension of tool use into new contexts may well be contested, resisted, or rejected.

One significant corollary of this view of tool use as culturally conditioned and as mediating human action is that the notion of 'skill' and
'ability' becomes to some extent rooted in its social location. This is
because the achievement of a goal is usually dependent on the use of tools
of one sort or another. The tools themselves can be imbued with 'skills',
which means the overall performance of human plus tool improves even
without change in the human's abilities. Shove *et al*. (2007) give the
example of developments in paint technology: 'smart paint' allows the
amateur to achieve results which only a skilled tradesperson could achieve
in the past. Therefore the ability to achieve goals depends at least as
much upon the use of specific tools, with skill distributed between human
and tool, as upon any innate abilities. As the tools change so will the
capabilities associated with them. In higher education, examples include
the development of structured VLEs, tools for planning sessions, and
presentation technologies.

'Skills' then are to an extent contextually contingent: they do not *only*
reside in the individual but in the individual-in-context: the tools that are
available, the job that is to be done. This is not to say that skills are never
transferable from context to context: as Wertsch points out (1998, p. 31),
having learned to ride one bicycle proficiently does not automatically limit
a person to riding that bicycle alone. But at the same time learning a skill
does not necessarily transfer to other forms of action with other material
objects.

Bringing the interrelationship of tool use and context into the equation casts some doubt on such concepts as 'core skills' and 'transferable
skills' and such practices as 'skills audits'. These notions are rooted in an
individualistic perspective which sees skills as residing within individuals
and as being relatively concrete, functionalist, cumulative, and context-
free. Adopting a sociocultural rather than a pychologistic level of analysis
re-frames the perspective on skills, focussing on their distribution between
the tools in use and the social context. Thus the 'skill' of lecturing, for
example, nowadays involves proficiency with tools such as PowerPoint,
itself involving facility with computers and their interface with projectors
as well as many subsidiary sets of knowledge and abilities associated with
computer use and the Windows or other interface. The skill of lecturing
emerges through the use of this set of mediational tools which influence
the development of the skill in particular instances.

Moreover, competence at lecturing and the efficiency of the learning
processes activated in any specific example of 'a lecture' will be conditioned by the specific character of the audience, the environment, the
course being followed, and the history of learning, relationships, and
expectations that led up to that point. Viewing the ability to lecture as
a personal skill alone is reductionist; by contrast, a 'connectionist' position links practice, individual agency, mediating cultural tools, and social

context. Connectionism foregrounds the social complexity of action into individual characteristics. In the memorable title of one of Clark's books (1997) it puts 'brain, body and world together again'.

Although we might not recognise them as such, in universities many of the tools we use are paper-based. Examples include assessment criteria pro formas, application forms, checklists, Quality Assurance Agency (QAA) codes of practice, and so on. Cooren (2004) suggests that such texts are agentic, which she defines as 'making a difference': the condition practices in certain ways. Actually, like other tools, they both reshape and are shaped by their context. I can illustrate this by contrasting the example of an assessment criteria pro forma with an example that Cooren gives (citing Bazerman, 1997, p. 296):

> The airline pilot's checklist before takeoff structures talk with the co-pilot, navigator, and ground crew; enacts directives from the legal and regulating bodies overseeing flight; establishes a record of actions taken by the flight crew; and provides a task-oriented frame for interpreting other recordings of conversations and instrument readings. Further, the checklist regularises and structures the procedures of the take-off, the perception and inspection of instruments and the physical environment, and the manipulation of the aircraft and its control.

In some ways the assessment pro forma performs similar functions. It structures how an assignment is read and how feedback is given; it enacts departmental and university assessment policy; it informs the student of what is required; it can serve to regularise and standardise assessment; and it can act as a standard for judgement. These functions actually are structural rather than, as Cooren argues, agentic; that is, they give regularity and predictability to social practice. However, as any academic will say, much of that description is aspirational rather than purely descriptive. Such pro formas are often ignored by staff and perhaps even more by students. Their contents are also subject to interpretation.

Referring to this difference between prescribed practices in tool use and those which actually happen, Brown and Duguid (1991) distinguish between 'canonical' and 'non-canonical' practices. Canonical practices are those set out in texts such as the pilot's checklist and the procedures associated with it set out in an operating manual. Non-canonical practice is what actually happens regardless of what the policy or manual states. Those close to the action have a considerable degree of discretion (Lipsky, 1980), and this is particularly true in universities where non-canonical practice is likely to be much more prevalent than in the cockpits of aircraft.

▶ Vignette: Tool use illustrated: Developments in modern languages teaching (adapted from Arthur and Klapper, 2000)

Arthur and Klapper (2000) describe the traditional approach to modern languages teaching as the grammar-translation method. This assumed that languages consisted of a collection of rules about words which could be readily described and learned. Teaching consisted of presentation of the rules (often through artificial constructions used for illustrative purposes such as 'la plume de ma tante'), while learning involved memorisation and application of the rules to language form. Here language learning was considered primarily a means of training the mind in rational thinking and problem solving. It also meant that language learning had a suitable place in universities. Tools in use here were largely textual: grammar, vocabulary lists, and dictionaries. This approach was dominant until well into the 1960s. It is still prevalent in some places in the world.

A second approach, the 'direct method', arose in the early part of the 20th century. Here the emphasis was on the spoken word, using only the language being learned. The development of the direct method occurred simultaneously with the spread of the new discipline of phonetics. The direct method assumed that second languages are learned in the same way as the native language and sought to reproduce the process of first language acquisition as far as possible. The intellectual components of the grammar-translation methods were thus largely lost. Tools here included flash cards and the immediate objects and people available in the classroom. This approach is still in use in many commercial language companies.

A third approach, 'audio-lingualism', developed after the Second World War. Here sophisticated tools such as language laboratories and tape recorders were used to facilitate drilling, the formation of habit, and the avoidance of grammatical or phonetic error. Based on behaviourist theory and now widely available recording technologies, the approach assumed that rewarding successful responses would encourage good learning and that repetition would instil successful performance in the future.

A fourth approach saw a shift from structural (with an emphasis on grammar and reproduction of performance) to generative approaches to language learning, ones that were more naturalistic and assumed that language production is a more creative process. The work of Chomsky (1957) underpinned this switch. He argued that children create new language that they have never learned or heard before because humans have an innate language faculty which allows them to discover, internalise, and then apply language rules in an inductive way. Research suggested that learners of second languages went through the same kind of processes, and in much the same order, as first language learners. Making mistakes became seen as a natural part of the language learning process: 'he goed' and 'we seed' represent the application of inductively derived rules which do not apply in these circumstances. Successful learners go beyond this stage to reach the ability to formulate the correct form, whether learning a first or a second language.

This generative approach led to the approach known as communicative language teaching (CLT), which focussed on the learner's need to learn language for particular purposes for use in particular contexts. Key features of CLT included awareness of cultural context, learner interaction, a focus on meaning, and the creative use of language through the application of inductively learned grammar. The tools in use then were learner interaction (sometimes in role plays) and authentic realia.

These changes have had important implications for the status of modern language teaching and learning in universities:

The fact that linguists themselves emphasise the need for a practical, skills-related approach has, at least in some quarters, relegated a hitherto respectable academic pursuit to one which operates a service function within higher education, much to the detriment of those who seek higher academic status (Arthur and Klapper, 2000, p. 103).

▶ **Commentary**

What, then, does this vignette tell us about tool use? It is clear that there are multiple factors conditioning the tools chosen for use in teaching and learning and where and how they are applied. They include the following:

- Political factors – for example, different positions on the place of modern languages in the university, the status of the discipline.
- Epistemological factors – for example, understandings about the nature of language and its use.
- Theories of learning – for example, understandings about what is needed to acquire a second language successfully and how that happens, and understandings of language acquisition founded in research.

- Ideological factors – for example, the educator's own position/s on these issues.
- Pragmatic factors – for example, the availability of technologies such as the language laboratory and the commercial needs and recruitment practices of commercial language schools.

Actual practices, including the use of tools, in relation to approaches to teaching and learning in specific contexts will be a subtle mix of these factors, a mix which will change over time and place.

If focussing *only* on the individual is essentialist and reductionist, so too is focussing *only* on the mediating tool. Like 'skills', tools need to be appreciated within their social contexts.

Domestication of initiatives

'Domestication' happens when workgroups engage with an initiative. That initiative accretes meaning and layers of significance in the doing of it. Some aspects acquire particular significance in this new context, other aspects drop away. Thus the initiative will be different in this context from any other – if the wheel is not exactly re-invented it is, at least, re-fashioned in new contexts. This can be very beneficial – it means that workgroups make the initiative their own. And a sense of ownership, as Fullan (1999) points out, is extremely helpful in change processes. Moreover, the re-fashioning process involved in domestication means the initiative is more likely to 'fit' the new context. Domestication can be a conscious or an unconscious process. Usually it is a combination of both. Because of it the results that initiatives for change lead to are different in different contexts. This makes things difficult for the top team who want to see initiatives through, or at least comply with external demands on them by introducing and enforcing a common set of practices.

Domestication as a process is extremely important for our understanding of policy. A formalistic understanding of policy sees it as consciously created in an intention-filled way by policy makers. From a sociocultural perspective policy is also created in the doing of it:

> Policy is . . . an 'economy of power', a set of technologies and practices which are realized and struggled over in local settings. Policy is both text and action, words and deeds, it is what is enacted as well as what is intended. Policies are always incomplete in so far as they relate to or map on to the 'wild profusion' of local practice. Policies are crude and simple. Practice is sophisticated, contingent, complex and unstable.
>
> (Ball, 1994, p. 10)

▶ **Vignette: Operation Blackboard, India: Domestication and the limits of centre–periphery change (adapted from Dyer, 1999)**

The Indian government's *National Policy on Education* (1986) identified three problems with primary education: alienation of the child; unsuitability of the formal structure of schooling for working children; and bareness of the school facilities. Operation Blackboard was the government's response. It promoted a child-centred approach to activity-based learning; launched a comprehensive system of non-formal education; and aimed at a substantial improvement in school facilities. Buildings would be extended, existing teachers trained in the new child-centred approaches to learning and the use of Operation Blackboard materials, new teachers employed, new methods and teaching and learning aids supplied and used. State governments had to submit plans and part-fund the project with national government. The plan was for the scheme to be fully operational within four years of inception (1990).

By 1992 there was only evidence of limited and patchy response: there were numerous and varied 'implementation gaps'. Building work had not been done, though foundations had sometimes been laid. In rural areas the plans for building extension under Operation Blackboard rooming norms were unnecessary – to build according to the plan would have been a waste of resources. New teachers had not been employed and materials remained unused, even unopened. The quality of the new materials was generally poor and their coverage of the curriculum incomplete, though they were to be found (usually stored away) in every primary school. Teachers took the poor quality of the kit as a symbol of the administration's lack of care for and interest in them. However, a few aids – the charts and abacus – were used quite widely by teachers.

Teachers had not been consulted about what the 'Blackboard' aids should be, and were surprised when they turned up. Though they had been 'trained' in their use they remained hazy about how and why they should be used. None of the training sessions had been synchronised with the arrival of the materials. With their unclear understanding, teachers generally thought that the innovation would involve them in extra work. Teachers' perceptions of their most immediate problems varied from area to area, but nowhere did Operation Blackboard address them. Only in those rural areas where there were no basic problems in the functioning of schools did Operation Blackboard find some acceptance. The policy initiative seemed to almost all teachers to have provided a remedy for the wrong ailment. None of them perceived themselves as having any stake in the changes aimed at by Operation Blackboard. The same was true for other key stakeholders: the Education Minister of Gujarat State saw the initiative as 'a frill' that might yield some resources which could be applied as 'a little embellishment here and there', and for which it was worth making 'the proper sounds'. A District Primary Officer predicted that the teaching and learning aids would find no use: 'these things conform to an ideal... with conditions where luxurious play material could be used'. By 1995, Operation Blackboard had become little more than a vigorous school-building programme.

► **Commentary**

It is clear from this vignette that planners did not take account of the diversity of need on the ground, of the importance of context. They diagnosed a fairly simple problem which, they assumed, was common throughout India. In fact there were different issues in different places, and the government 'solution' was not always appropriate. Moreover, it was domesticated even in those places where at least parts of it did address perceived need. This innovation was interpreted in extremely instrumental ways by those on the ground and even by regional officials: there was no ownership of it or the thinking underneath it.

In addition to this there is the more prosaic issue, that the management of change was not well planned; for example, the training sessions were not organised at the appropriate time.

► **Vignette: Electives at NewU: Policy reconstruction (adapted from Trowler, 1998)**

The University regulations [at NewU] require that 'electives' [modules that can be chosen by any student without prerequisites] be incorporated into programmes to broaden students' educational experience. It is also expected that programmes make some of their modules available to 'elective' students: non-specialists who study only one of these modules in the discipline. Both of these aspects of the principle of electives meet opposition from many academic staff because they are perceived to dilute student quality, make teaching more difficult and to reduce the ability to convey new subject content given that it becomes impossible to assume any prior knowledge. The elective programme, therefore, provides fertile ground for policy manipulation. One particularly inventive way of doing this was reported by one respondent who admitted that 'We actually cheat a little bit.' (35)

Staff made sure that the modules were known to be electives only by students in a particular discipline by putting them onto the computer after the course catalogue had been published, then taking them off the computer before the next catalogue was prepared. If this had not been done 'you just couldn't cope with the numbers' ... and the benefits of having students from this cognate discipline (who were already familiar with the background of the substantive content of the modules) would have been lost, as would potential later recruitment of some of them onto the degree programme of the area of study offering the elective. The effect was to make the programme appear 'legal' in terms of providing elective elements to the University yet to avoid suffering the consequences of just that.

Another, less complex strategy, was simply to inform Defined Field students that a particular module was the elective that they must take, thus creating an oxymoron: a compulsory elective.

(Trowler, 1998, pp. 131–132)

► Commentary

This vignette illustrates the subversion of institutional policy at local level, its domestication. Here the domestication was happening in quite deliberate ways. The policy was being interpreted and adapted to suit the needs and desires of the local department. Domestication is not always so consciously done, of course, but such deliberative actions are the easiest for the researcher to identify.

► Vignette: The Challenger launch decision (adapted from Vaughan, 1996)

Vaughan's book shows how the mistaken decision to launch the Challenger Shuttle (which exploded shortly after take-off due to faulty seals between its parts not functioning properly in cold weather) resulted from social structures at the meso level. Deviance within the organisation became transformed into socially acceptable behaviour and this led to a cultural predisposition to a response to conditions – a predisposition which would ultimately prove fatal. The rules on decision-making had become domesticated, but not in a good way.

Vaughan identifies a workgroup culture

> in which the managers and engineers working most closely on the [relevant part of the Shuttle seals problem] constructed beliefs and procedural responses that became routinized. The dominant belief...was that the [Shuttle] joints [and seals] were an acceptable risk: therefore it was safe to fly (p. 61).

A definition of the situation was developed which meant that 'to fly is safe despite this problem' and became the dominant way of seeing, and evidence to the contrary was ignored, largely because the shuttle had become seen as a kind of 'space bus' – a routine mode of space flight. Workgroups within both Thiokol (the makers of the relevant parts) and NASA had separately developed this approach to the problem and concluded that the solution was to find ways of working around the problem rather than opting for a thorough re-design, though for different reasons. The normalisation of deviance was possible because of the power of the workgroup culture.

> In interaction, workgroups create norms, beliefs, and procedures that are unique to their particular task. Although often far from harmonious, workgroups nonetheless do develop ways of proceeding and certain definitions of the situation that are shared and persist. These collectively constructed realities constitute the workgroup culture.
>
> (p. 64–65)

Ways of seeing develop incrementally in the gradual accrual of information, action, and definitions that shaped the workgroup's cultural construction of risk. This was invisible to participants because of the timescales involved, but the consistent directionality became apparent with hindsight. In the case of the Challenger launch decision, that culture had fatal consequences. In higher education the results are usually less devastating, but can be deleterious or beneficial depending on its character.

► Commentary

We know from studies such as that of Vaughan (1996) that the exercise of discretion and the development of non-canonical practice are often social in nature. New interpretations of rules and procedures develop and these lead to a domesticated version of what needs to be done. Vaughan's study showed how 'the normalisation of deviance' occurred as result of these social processes. In that case non-canonical practice, the domestication of safety procedures, and decision-making about them had deadly consequences.

The physical environment

Elaborating a little on the definition of social practice provided by Chouliaraki and Fairclough, Reckwitz suggests that social practice is

> a routinized type of behaviour which consists of several elements, interconnected to one other: forms of bodily activities, forms of mental activities, 'things' and their use, a background knowledge in the form of understanding, know-how, states of emotion and motivational knowledge.
>
> (Reckwitz, 2002, p. 249)

Thus the relationship between 'things', the environment, and the body are very relevant in conditioning social practice. The physical environment in which teaching and learning occurs has structural characteristics, imposing a certain degree of regularity on social practices, especially physical activity. Spaces and the things in them can configure activity, but at the same time there is co-adaptation of artefacts and practices (Latour, 2000). The design of buildings inside and out and their location both mirror practices (as the construction of banks did for financial practices that had developed prior their existence) and once built can begin to script, fossilise, them. The designs that are developed for our physical environment also mirror producers' and designers' theories of the relations between people, spaces, and things (Shove *et al.*, 2007).

It seems strange then that the physical environment is rarely taken into account in discussions of teaching and learning. The sub-discipline of eco-behaviourism (Barker, 1978) attempts to isolate the significance of the environment for individual behaviour, and adopts a psychological perspective in doing this. A sociocultural approach also sees architectural and environmental factors as significant in conditioning recurrent practices, but viewing through a social lens.

Many authors note the difficulties of establishing what the environmental effects are on individual social behaviour (Temple, 2007). Barker's early pioneering work was restricted to laboratory environments and very particular environmental conditions and behaviours. In reality, though behaviour, physical context and 'things', and their use (such as mobile learning technologies) all interact in complex ways that are difficult if not impossible to predict (Brown, 2005).

Trying to understand the significance of the physical environment is riven by multiple theoretical perspectives (Garling and Evans, 1991, p. 336), though almost all of them have been based on methodological individualism (MI) and rooted in psychology rather than sociology (Garling *et al.*, 1991, p. 342). The task of establishing any generalisations about environmental influences on behaviour is a hugely ambitious one, given the generality of the term 'environment' and of 'behavioural effects' as well as the problems of establishing causality.

Thinking about the physical environment of higher education has tended to stick to a few well-trodden paths:

> Consideration of space in higher education has commonly taken place either in the context of space planning, or in the context of campus master planning and architecture, rather than being seen as a resource to be managed as an integral part of teaching and learning, and research, activities. More recently, the idea of strategic planning of the university estate has emerged, linking decisions about the estate to wider issues of institutional strategy, but here the dominant concerns have been ones of space utilisation and financial effectiveness
>
> (Temple, 2007, pp. 10–11)

Every reflective educator knows how classroom layout, lighting, sound levels, and many other environmental factors can affect the dynamics of the teaching and learning experience. Innovative spaces such as the Learning Grid and Reinvention Centre at the University of Warwick (see pp. 74–75) or the Learning Gateway at the University of Cumbria address such issues in carefully thought-out ways. By contrast, anyone who has tried to conduct participative learning experiences or workshops in tiered lecture theatres which have clearly been designed with a particular model of higher education in mind also knows how constraining the contrast between the original architect's preconceptions and the present-day intentions can be. This is an example of 'distributed cognition', the view that 'knowing' involves more than simply what is in people's heads, but unfortunately too often works against the goal of effective teaching and learning.

Beyond the classroom, ecological effects are important too, the presence or absence of a staff common room, the flow of people along corridors, the allocation of workrooms to individuals or groups, the location of administrators in relation to academics, the design of the university, and – most significantly – whether it is on a campus or distributed across the city. All have very significant effects on the social dynamics of teaching and learning and on community-building, as Temple's review of the literature showed:

> There is a broad acceptance in the literature that the design of the 'the learning landscape', around the campus and within buildings, can help to create a sense of belonging, as well as facilitating peer group discussion and thus informal learning. These social features of higher education appear to be bound up with student retention and progression in complex ways. Many of the physical features, inside and outside buildings, which are thought to support these benefits are small-scale and low-cost.
>
> (Temple, 2007, p. 5)

Unfortunately, this 'broad acceptance' has not been translated into clear and well-substantiated detailed proposals for how best to achieve these beneficial effects.

In an earlier study (Trowler and Turner, 2002) I noted that academics new to the department were inducted more by serendipitous interactions within the department than by any formal induction provision. Overheard conversations, chance meetings over the photocopier, and coffee room chats tended to be the ways in which neophytes picked up the significant dynamics of the regime they had entered. Such 'under the stage' interactions are highly significant, and they are precisely the ones that are most affected by ecological conditions because they are unplanned. In another study (Trowler and Knight, 2001), respondents told us how they noticed the effects of departmental layout, because they were able to compare what were for them novel aspects of this with their previous experiences. For example, one told us,

> In actual fact this corridor, I think, is made up of people who have worked together quite closely from number of years and they are all in that same field. There are a lot of telecommunications people in this corridor and they have a sort of subgroup . . . I think they have quite a cohesive group of people there.

The effects are iterative rather than one way, however. In other words, social processes and the nature of local cultures in particular locales condition the way that spaces and places are used. Design intentions may be undermined by the actual use made of rooms: changes may be made to layouts; common rooms may be used for other purposes than those intended; and workarounds may be found when the environment structures our behaviour in ways which are unwelcome to individuals or groups. Structure and agency are both in operation therefore, spaces and objects are not fixed, their social significance and their relation to social practice are always dynamic.

▶ Vignette: Space policy (from observant participation)

A faculty policy and resources committee was discussing the proposal from the faculty's postgraduate committee of the university that MA students might be allocated a room of their own in each department in which to socialise and study. A range of views were expressed. Some departmental representatives pointed out that in the past such a room had existed in their department but the provision had created problems of various sorts. Others, though, pointed out that there was a contradiction between the university wanting to attract many more students and yet not providing dedicated facilities for them.

Finally, a member of the committee pointed out that in a new Business Faculty building in another part of the campus (a different faculty from this committee's) there were open spaces and open access rooms for everyone. Many rooms had glass sides opening onto a general concourse with tables and a coffee shop. The result was 'a real buzz of activity and the feeling of a lot going on'. That building had free wireless Internet access, and students could be seen conversing in person while simultaneously accessing the Internet on their laptops to retrieve information or to involve others in virtual dialogue. Students of all sorts and levels of study could be seen talking together, sharing ideas, and socialising in this new building.

In concluding his description of this new building the committee member made his point – that the idea of providing rooming resources dedicated to particular groups of students was outdated and counterproductive. His observations drew the agreement of the whole committee, and a resolution was passed to propose such general access spaces in the new developments taking place in that part of the campus.

▶ Commentary

The interesting thing about this vignette is the way that the discourse prior to that person's intervention had been structured around the notion of the MA course and whether or not to provide a dedicated room for 'that type of student'. The discussion was limited conceptually and discursively by the history of the institution and by its current rooming policies, setting out different space allocations for different categories of user, in that older part of the campus. In that part of campus there still existed, for example, junior common rooms and senior common rooms, and departments were oriented around cell-like spaces for both postgraduate students and academic staff with very little public space available. There was no wi-fi facility available there. Tools (such as wi-fi), architecture, history, and discourse intertwined in this discussion in a mutually reinforcing way. Yet one intervention could serve to break the discourse and illuminate a new way of seeing.

▶ Vignette: Higher education managers reshape the environment (adapted from Prichard, 2000 and Tierney, 1987)

A Dean at 'Southern University' was concerned that managerialist developments at his university were reducing the social contacts between staff, who increasingly stayed in their individual offices or worked from home in order to meet the increasing demands made of them and their time. The close interactions between staff and students were also being reduced in this more pressurised environment. In order to counter this tendency set about changing the use of office space to create what he termed a 'freeway' of students and staff he deliberately had. . . .

> a couple of teaching rooms and a research room there (next door) and a photocopier there to make it into a little freeway, a photocopy machine and a common room down the hall and very often I can sit in on chats with the people there. If I'm not having a conversation like this (with researcher) and I'm not desperate to do something that requires my full concentration, then I keep the door open and people pop in and have a chat.
>
> (Prichard, 2000, p. 140)

However, managers' intentions are not always received and put into practice in the way they expected. Tierney (1987) recounts the story of how a new college principal – Sister Vera – also decided to implement an open-door policy. She literally left her office door open as a symbol of her accessibility and democratic leadership. However, the previous incumbent of the post of principal of the small Catholic college in the United States used to walk around the college greeting the staff by name and chatting about their families and interests. Having been there for decades, she knew the staff intimately and had a warm relationship with them. By contrast, Sister Vera entered the college via the corridor within which her room was located, looked straight ahead, walked into her office, and greeted her secretary. In this context, with this history, the simple ploy of leaving the office door open could not shift the perception that here was a managerialist and cold principal. Indeed, the reverse was the case: the open door became a symbol of Sister Vera's callous attempts to manipulate staff attitudes, a sign of cynicism and the failure of communication.

► Commentary

The point of this brief vignette is that managers' perceptions and intentions are sometimes very different from the perceptions and 'reading' of those they seek to lead. The message sent is not always the message received; indeed it is probably rarely so. Rather than expecting the message to be received in the same state it was sent, it is important to expect that this will in most cases 'not' be the case, and to consider the possible or probable reinterpretations that will occur as the message is decoded 'on the ground'.

The backstory

> Insofar as organizations have a history of which they themselves are products, signs cannot be adequately understood if we do not first comprehend the historical processes in which the signs are produced and embedded
>
> (Tierney, 1987, p. 235)

> In this great future, you can't forget your past (Bob Marley, *No Woman No Cry*).

The backstory is the mosaic of narratives about the history that lies behind the current situation which is the actual focus of attention. The idea of backstory as used here is distinguished from 'history' in that it is not necessarily a *factual* account of historical background. Rather, it refers to the narratives told about that history. Narratives are very selective retrospective accounts which tend to be simplified and linear and which have the eventual achievement or punchline functioning as the goal to be reached from the beginning. There are usually a number of steps in this: 'the stages of a journey along the path that had been visible from the beginning' (Deuten and Rip, 2000, p. 71).

The significance of conceptualising the backstory is to lend historicity to an understanding of where people are now and how that conditions the reception and understanding of new developments and how it shapes and limits their actions. Shils says,

> Every human action and belief has a career behind it, it is the momentary end-state of a sequence of transmissions and modifications and their adaptation to current circumstance. Although everyone bears a great deal of past achievement in his belief and conduct, there are many persons who fail to see this.
>
> (Shils, 1981, p. 43)

But, as Feldman and Feldman (2006) point out, the same is true of collectives:

> Every act of organizational remembering has a career: it is specific to the time in which it occurs, connected to past and future acts of remembering, thus enacting a chain of remembering.

The narratives on which this remembering is based are developed locally and parts of them may be received from wider cultural sources. They are malleable, and may change as circumstances change, and they are re-shaped for different audiences (Deuten and Rip, 2000). There is a relationship between events at the foreground and the version of the backstory that is told. In the South African context there is a strong and wide-ranging backstory, for example. It encompasses a national higher education context oriented around the concept of 'transformation', which means many things to South Africans but most of all the idea that there is a need to remake social institutions to encompass previously very disadvantaged racial groups. The broader backstory also encompasses the story of apartheid. That story has been remade in many South African contexts so that today it is almost impossible to find anyone who supported that regime and there are many people who tell stories of their part, or more usually the part of others who are close to them, in the struggle against apartheid. These proximal and distal dimensions of the backstory touch on many issues of daily life and professional practice in South Africa, including issues around teaching and learning within universities, especially as they relate to the inclusion of black, coloured, and Indian populations (racial categories still used in South Africa today). Backstories are more local too, relating to the 'organizational saga' (Clark, 1972), to personalities and events within the institution and within the organisational subunits. Even at this local level the backstory is malleable.

► Conclusion

This chapter has set the analysis of departmental and sub-departmental practices in relation to teaching and learning within the context of socio-cultural theory generally. Viewing teaching and learning in relation to recurrent practices in a social rather than a purely individual context enables us to focus on the relevance of both structure and agency in everyday life within universities. Structures impose regularity and a degree of predictability on what we do, yet at the same time we have agency as individuals and as members of groups. Patterned behaviour is evident from place to place, yet in each place the patterns grow up to be different in important ways despite important contextual similarities. Newcomers to a context face challenges in acclimatising to, and sometime shifting, these patterns, but once there they become an important new element in the social mix, bringing with them sometimes new cultural elements from outside. The next chapter explores in more detail cultures at the meso level in universities, in workgroups and departments.

3   Teaching and Learning Regimes: A Brief Overview

▶ Why 'teaching and learning' regimes?

As I explained at the end of the previous chapter, the focus now moves from the organisational level to a more local level of analysis: workgroups within departments in universities. The aim is to unpick the nature of cultures there and in particular to examine the ways in which a cultural perspective might assist in efforts to enhance teaching and learning. The argument is that workgroups which engage together on common projects over extended periods of time develop a set of contextually specific characteristics which could be described as a culture or a subculture. However, I prefer to use the word 'regime' when the 'culture' concept is applied to a specific issue such as teaching and learning.

Though the focus here is on teaching and learning (and assessment, and curriculum) regimes, equally there are research regimes and leadership regimes, for example, with somewhat different constituent 'moments' (a concept I elaborate later). The focus on teaching and learning regimes, then, is a choice, not a necessary characteristic.

The first health warning (one of several in the book) is to draw attention to one problem in putting the emphasis on teaching and learning practices at the meso level. That is, that doing so draws a line between local practices, values, attitudes, and assumptions on the one hand and their wider policy and socio-economic environment on the other. Practices are intimately connected to their context. 'Regimes' are porous, leaky. There is a flow into them, through them, and out again into the wider environment.

The context of higher education has changed fundamentally worldwide in the last decade of the 20th century and into the 21st century. Managerialism, economic pressures on HE, and the changing nature of the student body have, among other broader conditions, continued to exert significant pressures on teaching and learning practices, on what is possible, on what works. The danger in focussing on teaching and learning practices in HE is that these wider factors will be bracketed out. So it is important to remember that regimes are both agentic and structurally conditioned, that their characteristics are both constructed and enacted.

They are open, natural systems, and any 'boundaries' are more analytical and subjective constructs than in any sense 'real'.

▶ Why 'regime'?

The word 'regime' comes from the Latin *regimen* (from *regere*, meaning to rule/to govern). It is usually used to describe the way a political system operates (democratic, totalitarian). Its use in this book is perhaps closer to the French meaning than the English. In French it acquired a broader meaning in the early 19th century as the bundle of rules constitutive of a specific (non-political) institution – for example, 'regime fiscal', 'regime matrimonial', and so on. By extension, it came to describe the way a system operates through regulation/agreements to shape a phenomenon or activity. It also has a technical meaning which describes the way in which certain physical/mechanical phenomena occur (le regime d'un moteur de voiture). The way it is used here is derivative of that broader meaning of how a system operates to shape an activity, and describes the system (made up of complex and tenuous elements) that circumscribes the interactions, beliefs, and behaviours of a group. The word 'regime' describes that which can be seen at the surface, and implies underpinning sets of rules/components that are not visible.

The term also evokes the idea of *political regimes* not only with the connotations of the use of power and of the dominance of a way of seeing the world, but in a context of resistance and contest. Similarly, for those in the medical profession it evokes the idea of *treatment regime* – an attempt to address and cure a condition, again not only backed by the power of doctors and the medical profession but with the possibility of alternatives and of non-compliance. As Foucault says, 'where there is power there is resistance' (1990, p. 95). In teaching and learning regimes, both power and resistance can operate. They are often sites of contest between competing ways of seeing and doing.

One reason for the choice of that word is to be deliberately provocative. While the currently popular term 'community' (. . . of practice) has connotations of consensus and harmony, 'regime' has these overtones of oppression, power, and, usually, resistance and conflict. Indeed, both the terms 'culture' and 'community' (of practice) involve ideas of mutuality, of shared norms and values, of practices based on consensus: the Kezar and Eckel (2002) example of this was cited in the previous chapter.

There is an element of functionalism in this way of thinking, the assumption that consensus is privileged over difference, that consensus is somehow 'normal' and beneficial to the whole community while conflict is just 'dazzle' (Fox, 1980). Wenger *et al.*, 2002, do go some way to acknowledging this point, that conflict is often endemic and in fact can in some cases be a positive influence in that it leads to change which has beneficial effects. The notion of regime helps us problematise those ideas which are rooted in the functionalist tradition, picturing, as they do, the status quo as a smooth-running machine operating for the general good.

In discussing teaching and learning regimes it is very easy to slip into thinking of them as bounded groups with particular configurations of understandings, similar practices, and sets of values. Much of the literature about social practice tends to do this. The word 'community' in 'community of practice' (Wenger, 1998) suggests boundedness as does 'system' in the phrase 'activity system' (Engestrom, 2001). If teaching and learning regimes do constitute a system, then they are open, natural systems; highly permeable, vertically nested, and horizontally multiple. Where there are boundaries these are usually either analytical (a choice made by the researcher to categorise) or subjective (participants making distinctions between 'us' and 'them').

Moreover, different issues split teaching and learning regimes in different ways: in universities, issues such as the different priority that should be given to teaching versus research, to widening participation versus selecting the 'best' students, may cleave a workgroup differently. Yet, while there may be sometimes acrimonious debate about big issues such as these, subterranean smaller issues may find consensus: that postgraduate teaching assistants should be used in the first year of an undergraduate degree but not afterwards, for example (see p. 94 for an elaboration).

While 'communities of practice' theory assumes at least a certain degree of intersubjectivity – a common set of understandings and meanings shared between group members which render full articulation of meaning between them unnecessary – this assumption is not made here. On some issues at some times there may be intersubjectivity, but under no circumstances can it be taken for granted.

Teaching and learning regimes, therefore, often constitute sites of contest as well as consensus. How far they are consensual and how far their terrain is contested will differ from site to site and from time to time. Sometimes, a highly bounded, highly consensual TLR may exist in fact as well as analytically; something closer to the community of practice as described by Lave and Wenger (1991), and by Wenger (1998) in particular:

[Individuals in] . . . a community of practice . . . make the job possible by inventing and maintaining ways of squaring institutional demands with the shifting realities of actual situations. Their practice:

1) provides resolutions to institutionally generated conflicts...
2) supports a communal memory that allows individuals to do their work without needing to know everything
3) helps newcomers join the community by participating in practice
4) generates specific perspectives and terms to enable accomplishing what needs to be done
5) makes the job habitable by creating an atmosphere in which the monotonous and meaningless aspects of the job are woven into the rituals, customs, stories, events, dramas and rhythms of community life.

(Wenger, 1998, p. 46)

When this happens a number of factors have usually been in place:

- The workgroup is of small-enough size to permit relatively frequent interaction between its members.
- The group or its leader has been able to select its members, rather than this being done exogenously.
- The group membership shares one or more important structural features in common (for example, gender, ethnicity, or social class)

However even in highly consensual workgroups there is only provisional stability: consensus for now.

But the concept of regime is not intended to relate to the Foucauldian notion of 'truth regimes'. That concept implies the hegemony of one way of seeing the world, the discursive exclusion of alternative ways of seeing and describing 'reality'. Such a view is certainly too structuralist (in the sense of seeing society as determining and dominating the individual's behaviour and thoughts). What we often see on the ground in higher education is contest and tension as well as stability and consensus, imposed or not. Neither characteristic, contest or consensus, is permanent of course: both mutate over time.

Teaching and learning regimes: The parts

A teaching and learning regime can be analytically deconstructed into a constellation of eight constituent parts, which I will refer to as 'moments'. This term is used in order to situate society, and the nature of cultures within it, in the following way (these comments are based on Harvey, 1996). First, the social world is dynamic – in a constant state of creation and change. Second, individuals within it are both free and constrained: both the subject and the object of the social world, that is its creator and that which is created by it. Issues of 'scale', of level of analysis, are important in this. The social world looks different depending on where one places the analytical focus. Focussing at more macro levels tends to emphasise structure, determination, and regularities. Closer focus tends to emphasise the power of individuals, their agency, and nuanced differences. A low-level focus emphasises the parts, while a high-level focus emphasises the whole. Because the social whole is greater than the sum of its parts, and because the parts are less than the whole, something is missed wherever one chooses to place the focus of analysis. Analytical boundaries are therefore created (and destroyed) by the choice of scale.

The eight moments have been abstracted by analysing relevant literature and from my empirical work on cultures and change in higher education. The publications are listed in the References. Taken together, the eight moments involve the following:

1. sets of practices that are habitual and taken for granted
2. sets of tacit assumptions about what constitutes 'normal' behaviour
3. implicit theories about students, teaching, and learning
4. ways of expressing oneself and interpreting the words of others
5. conventions about appropriate and inappropriate practices in teaching and learning contexts
6. the flow of power relations
7. the creation of the 'self' in relation to others
8. attributions of meaning and affect to ideas, practices, and institutions

In different combinations and in interaction, these constitute a teaching and learning regime.

In some senses these moments of a TLR share some characteristics of Bourdieu's notion of habitus, a set of dispositions, perceptions, and actions which give people who are immersed in them a 'feel for the game', an intuitive understanding of what is 'right', even in the absence of explicit rules or procedures. Individuals both construct and enact the context they exist in so that there is mutuality of influence in operation, not simple structural determination by outside forces.

Teaching and learning regimes: The whole

'Seeing' a teaching and learning regime involves abstracting from the complexity of social reality particular characteristics which are of analytical interest. Other characteristics become hidden in this process of abstraction. In this sense, teaching and learning regimes are an example of an *ideal type* in Weber's notion: an analytical construct rather than a description of 'reality'. They are a figure set within its contextual ground. But what constitutes figure and what constitutes ground is a matter of analytical choice, conditional on the lens chosen and the object of interest. Bourdieu (1977, p. 29) has warned us against mistaking our chosen model of reality and the reality of the model. He is right to do so: focussing on teaching and learning regimes is to take only part of 'reality' and abstract it from the rest, looking at it in ways conditioned by analytical constructs. Doing so can offer illumination, but there is a danger of distortion for the unwary.

To concretise this discussion in terms of the issue at hand, teaching and learning regimes are analytical abstractions from contexts in which groups work together on a common project – involving teaching and learning – over an extended period of time. Other things are going on; for example, the higher education system is changing in fundamental ways in the United Kingdom because of massification, the increasing significance of student fees, and the push for widened participation. These are macro trends and have structural properties which affect cultures on the ground in very significant ways. However, the 'regimes' concept focuses on key objects of interest when the intention is to develop and improve practices to do with learning, teaching, assessment, and curriculum. This is a way of depicting a unique context of interrelationships, tensions, and power flows which adds to the usually adopted levels of analysis: the individual teacher and individual student, on the one hand, and at the organisational or system level, on the other.

If teaching and learning regimes are the figure, then what constitutes the ground? In relation to changes in teaching and learning practices in universities some of the following factors are very significant: the characteristics of leadership both locally and institutionally; the different competing agendas that exist in a particular context; the nature and impact of 'Great Culture' (Alvesson, 2002) on local contexts (that is broader structural characteristics including national cultures); the nature of the institution in which teaching and learning regimes are manifested and the corporate culture there; and finally, disciplines and narratives about disciplines and of teaching and learning within them.

Malcolm Tight (2004) conducted an extensive content analysis study of research into higher education and published about higher education in 284 books and in 406 articles in 17 journals published in 2000. In relation to the level of analysis adopted he says the following about this literature:

Seven levels of analysis were identified, ranging from the individual through the course, department, institution, nation and system (i.e. an idealised, unspecified nation) to the international. Of these, research was most commonly focused on the national level.

(p. 397)

What is interesting about Tight's findings for our purposes is that only 18 of the 406 articles adopted the departmental level of analysis. Less than half of these had any theoretical content, being descriptive only. There is clearly, then, a need to rebalance thinking in this area and to add the meso-level analysis to the dominant ones.

Cultures, regimes, and the significance of structure

The significant difference between 'teaching and learning cultures' (TLC) as normally understood and 'teaching and learning regimes' (TLR) is that the latter concept incorporates the former but additionally includes contextual characteristics beyond the norms, values, attitudes, and taken-for-granted knowledge of social groups (Bloomer and James, 2001, though, adopt a definition of TLC close to this, as do Hodkinson and James, 2003). By 'contextual characteristics' I mean the legacies of the specific history of that group, the issues it is currently engaging with, the particular types of students being taught, the specific challenges the group faces, and the affordances available to the group. These contextual characteristics are structural in nature, lending coherence and relative permanence to social practices in different times and locales. (Giddens, 1984). It is these characteristics, rather than any simple homogeneity within the culture of the group, that lend coherence to teaching and learning regimes. The notion of 'regime', then, places more stress on diversity, conflict, power, and dynamism than do the concepts of either 'culture' or 'community (of practice)'.

A similar point is made about activity theory by Rodriguez:

Context is constituted through the enactment of activity involving people and artefacts... (which) carry with them a particular culture and history and are persistent structures that stretch across activities through time and space. Context is both internal to people and at the same time external.... The crucial point is that in activity theory external and internal are fused, unified.

(Rodriguez, 1998)

In distinction to the notion of a 'culture of teaching and learning', there is no presumption of shared values and attitudes across the whole group within the idea of a 'regime'. However, it is the common context that gives distinctiveness to the cultural characteristics and sets the framework within which diversity flourishes. Thus there may be conflict and tension over questions of identity and competing ideas about what constitutes 'appropriateness'. Yet these tensions and contradictions operate within a common framework that defines and sets the parameters for debate.

As I stressed earlier, the moments of culture do need to be understood holistically, and are only separated here for analytical purposes. Without such separation the concept of culture becomes jelly-like. But it is not only the moments of teaching and learning regimes that need to be considered both together and separately. So too do culture and culture's context. If culture is understood as a particular configuration of the moments of social life in a particular place and space, then regime is that constellation as it is mobilised in relation to a given area of activity, towards a given subject (for example, particular students) with a given historical background, with particular tools and capacities, and in the context of a given social framework.

This means, as James and Bloomer eloquently put it (2001, p. 7),

> Research and scholarship must recognise learning not simply as occurring within the cultural context but as a cultural practice. It must take as its focus the practices of people in their authentic learning sites and avoid the alchemy that so readily turns students and teachers in two instances of a category, into a species, or alternatively has them as the mere carriers of culture or cognitive operations.

Teaching and learning regimes: A figure in its ground

It is best to see a teaching and learning regime as the figure in its ground, as a choice of subject on which to focus, and a consequent choice to de-focus other areas. I have selected this particular figure for this book because I am interested in cultural construction at the departmental level in universities and its significance for teaching and learning. Clearly, other figures, alternative places for the spotlight of attention to fall, could have been chosen.

If teaching and learning regimes are the figure then their significant ground involves a mix of other characteristics which have important effects upon the other operation. They include the leadership characteristics of the department and the institution in which workgroups operate. In a heavily top-down and authoritarian context the significance of backstage and under-the-stage talk and practices is increased. These terms, mentioned briefly earlier, refer to the articulation of culture on different 'stages' or arenas (Goffman, 1959; Bailey, 1977; Becher, 1988). There is the public arena, front-of-stage, in which formal proclamations about values and practices are made in, for example, mission statements and speeches by vice chancellors. This front-of-stage presentation may have little to do with actual practices, values, attitudes, and meanings on the ground, though it is not without effect and can have important repercussions on 'corporate culture', even though hardly touching culture as understood sociologically in an organisation. The backstage arena is where deals are done: individuals and small groups make decisions and take actions away from the public eye. These often have very significant implications for the social life of institutions. Finally, under-the-stage arena is where gossip is purveyed, nicknames are used, stories are told, and jokes and critical comments are exchanged. Coffee bars, common rooms, private offices, and even public spaces (hushed tones over the photocopier) tend to be the venues for the articulation of culture under-the-stage. One could refer to this as a 'counter-culture', but this takes it too far: under-the-stage phenomena are, in essence, a particular 'take' on practices, subjectivities, assumptions, and so on that are part of participants' everyday lives.

In authoritarian contexts, to repeat, the under-the-stage arena becomes particularly significant. In such contexts too there appears to be less room for discretion, although in reality workgroups will invariably develop unique practices even in a highly regulated environment (Roberts et al., 1994, conducted studies of naval practices on nuclear-powered aircraft carriers which demonstrate this).

A second characteristic of the 'ground' is the nature and number of competing agendas that exist there: in other words, what the significant issues are for a workgroup within a university. Where the issues are few and relatively uncontentious then there is more chance of the workgroup having at least some of the characteristics of a 'community of practice', a consensual social group. However, it is more likely that there are numerous agendas in play and some of them will be contentious. Where this is the case the workgroup will be split along different lines according to each issue, split one way in relation to the priority that should be given to teaching as against research and another in relation to priorities given to income generation or widening participation, for example. Sometimes it is easier to see conflict over big issues and so remain unaware of corresponding consensus over small ones.

A third characteristic relates to the nature of the institution itself: whether it is multi-campus or single-campus university; whether it is an elite 'selecting' institution or a 'recruiting' one; what its staff recruitment policies are and whether there is a high staff turnover; and what the general morale of academic staff is at the time. Beyond this is the significance of the broader national cultural environment, what Alvesson (2002) calls 'Great Culture'. This is discussed in more detail on pp. 13 and 23.

▶ Conclusion

Teaching and learning regimes are depictions of unique constellations of sets of practices and frameworks of meaning oriented to teaching and learning projects in particular higher education situations. TLRs evolve through the interactions within workgroups over an extended period of engagement with their projects. They are open, natural systems and as such are conditioned by structural forces in the wider context. The meanings workgroups attribute to their projects and the ways they define their situation are themselves partly formulated within the regime that develops. Meanings and intentions are not always shared, though: there are dynamic tensions around subjectivities, alternative sets of meanings, competing sets of practices, and power relations. Teaching and learning regimes are almost always sites of contest. However, there is often a degree of consensus too (usually taken for granted among participants) and, crucially, a shared social context in which these tensions are played out.

In terms of the messages for practice, a spotlight on the development and enactment of cultures at the workgroup level is significant because of the following facts:

- It illuminates the significance of current assumptions, conventions and practices, which are always significant when attempting to introduce new ones.
- It helps those on the ground to think about their own context.
- It helps explain why attempts to improve things sometimes work and sometimes do not (see, for example, Trowler and Cooper, 2002).

4 Teaching and Learning Regimes Deconstructed

I've come to see that – just as 'all politics is local' – on most campuses there are in fact dozens of microenvironments with sharply divergent cultures: good-spirited, productive departments coexist along-side dysfunctional ones. As a faculty member once explained to me: 'When we go to work in the morning, we go to our department.'

(Marchese, 1999, p. vii)

Institutionalized belief systems – the framework of rules, roles and authority relations – affect choice by generating cultural scripts according to which certain social relationships and actions are taken-for-granted. They stand as common understandings, deeply embedded, seldom explicitly articulated. The patterns found in much social life derive from the taken-for-granted quality of these institutionalized cultural scripts, which are then reproduced in other structures.

(Vaughan, 1996, p. 197)

▶ Introduction: The nature of the eight moments

This chapter unpacks the concept of teaching and learning regimes. Wuthnow makes the point that the closely related concept of *culture* is a very slippery one:

Culture is, assuredly, a perplexing phenomenon and ubiquitous in presence, complex in detail, and as such overwhelming and incomprehensible in its totality and in its intricacy. Any attempts to grasp it all in analysis will, therefore, be frustrated from beginning to end.

(Wuthnow *et al.*, 1987, p. 71)

Words like 'culture', unless deconstructed or disaggregated, are in great danger of becoming meaningless. The well-known social commentator

Raymond Williams is reported to have said, 'I don't know how many times I've wished that I had never heard the damned word' (quoted in Kuper, 2001, p. 1). Wertsch (1991) is right that culture is a process, and the 'things' that appear in list-like definitions of cultures are merely residua of that process.

Yet, as archaeologists know well, the identification of residua is important: accounts can be constructed with what has been left behind, and sometimes that is all you have. In deconstructing an idea that is close to 'culture', I don't wish to oversimplify or suggest that each disaggregated part exists independently. The purpose of the exercise is simply to lend some analytical purchase to the concept of teaching and learning regimes. In my view it is helpful to consider separately the eight moments broadly identified in Chapter 3, despite Wertsch's warnings. They are, to recap, recurrent practices; tacit assumptions; implicit theories of teaching and learning; discursive repertoires; conventions of appropriateness; power relations; subjectivities in interaction; and codes of signification. These eight moments could be used to disaggregate the concept of 'culture' in general, as the first vignette of this chapter illustrates.

However, the health warning mentioned earlier should always be in place: while considering them separately for analytical purposes, these moments are in a relationship of articulation (Laclau and Moufee, 1985) with each other – one of shifting mutuality of relationship, sometimes hardening and then becoming dynamic again. Commenting on Harvey's six moments,[3] Chouliaraki and Fairclough (1999, p. 6) make exactly this point:

> Each moment internalises all of the others – so that discourse is a form of power, a mode of formation of beliefs/values/desires, an institution, a mode of social relating, a material practice. Conversely, power, social relations, material practices, institutions, beliefs, etc. are in part discourse. The heterogeneity within each moment – including discourse – reflects its simultaneous determination . . . by all other moments.

▶ Vignette: The Bookseller of Kabul (Seierstad, 2004) – an illustration of cultural 'moments'

Norwegian journalist Seierstad lived with the family of Sultan Khan in Kabul in the spring of 2001. She describes herself as living as a 'bi-gendered' creature, a woman who was allowed access to the lives of men and women in ways that women in Afghanistan normally are not.

Khan had run his bookshops during the Taliban regime, which had recently fallen. This fundamentalist Muslim government had banned the use of images of living creatures and his bookshops were periodically raided and books which contained these were destroyed. Khan had devised numerous ways to avoid his books being burned or defaced by the Taliban: he covered the pictures with business cards and hid those books he could not bear to deface in this way. He loved books, and though a devout Muslim had no problem with these images.

But the fall of the Taliban regime created a business opportunity for Khan. School textbooks needed to be created for the schoolchildren of the new regime and Khan wanted to print them:

When the schools open this spring there will hardly be any textbooks. Books printed by the Mujahedeen government and the Taliban are useless. This is how first-year schoolchildren learn the alphabet: J is Jihad our aim in life, I is for Israel, our enemy, K. is for Kalashnikov, we will overcome...War was the central theme in maths books too. Schoolboys – because the Taliban printed books solely for boys – did not calculate in apples and cakes, but in bullets and Kalashnikovs. Something like this: 'little Omar has a Kalashnikov with three magazines. There are 20 bullets in each magazine. He uses two thirds of the bullets and kills 60 infidels. How many infidels does he kill with each bullet?' (p. 62)	*Discursive Repertoires*

(continued)

Seierstad describes how males dominated life in Afghan culture. Sultan Khan as the head of household ruled the family members autocratically. His son and younger brother were forced, very reluctantly, to work for him in his bookshops. This caused great resentment among them.	*Power Relations*
Afghanistan being a traditionally polygamous culture, Khan took a second, younger wife. Although accepted by her, this caused shame and unhappiness for his first wife. This was particularly the case because most men with two wives tried to keep a balance in the relationship, spending one night with one wife and the next with the other. They made sure to give them equal amounts of clothes and gifts. But Khan's wife, Sharifa, felt rejected. She was once the respected wife of a bookseller, an entrepreneur. She was the mother of his sons and daughters, respected for that too. But now she felt shamed and ashamed, hated him for ruining her life and for having taken away her children.	*Subjectivities in Interaction*
The women in household, like all women in that culture, were not allowed to meet men beyond the family on their own, wore the burka which covered them from head to toe, their face behind a grill, and needed to be accompanied by a male when they ventured out in public.	*Conventions of Appropriateness*
Many resented these limitations placed on them, but underneath the burka many wore make-up. Their shoes became highly significant when they went out because their shoes were the only part of them visible beneath the burka. The shoes became highly symbolic and very important to the women.	*Codes of Signification*
The burka failed in other ways to fulfil the functions planned by its male designers. Describing the interaction between a burkawearer and a shopkeeper, Seierstad writes,	*Power relations (challenging)*

Shakila rocks her head to and fro, smiles roguishly and laughs, she haggles, yes, she even flirts. Under the sky-blue one can detect her coquettish game. She has been doing it all along. . . . She can flirt with her little finger, with a foot, the movement of a hand . . . And the vendor can decipher the moods of a waving, nodding, billowing burka with ease (p. 90)

Seierstad relates the story of Saliqa, who transgressed these rules and met a boy alone, but doing no more than talking to him. When her deviance became known she was physically attacked by members of her family and imprisoned in her room. Her mother wailed that Saliga had disgraced the family. Longing for love was taboo, forbidden by notions of honour and by the mullahs. Young people cannot meet alone, and they cannot choose who to love, or even to love at all.

Power relations

To all appearances there is no sex life in Afghanistan. Women hide behind the burka, and under the burka they wear large, loose clothes. Under the skirts they wear long trousers and even within the four walls of the house low-necked garments are a rarity. Men and women who do not belong to the same family must not sit together in the same room. They must not talk to each other or eat together. In the countryside even the weddings are segregated; the women dance and make merry and so do the men, in different rooms. But under the surface all is seething. In spite of running the risk of the death penalty, in Afghanistan too people have lovers and mistresses. There are prostitutes in the towns to whom young boys and men can resort while they wait for a bride." (p.56)

Recurrent Practices

(continued)

But Seierstad tells the story too of Leila, who wants an education. She has to sneak to the school for her first English lesson without her father or mother knowing. But she finds herself in a classroom with boys, and she cannot wear a burka in the classroom. She has to expose her face to the boys and feels she is turning her soul inside out. The experience makes her feel dirty, exposed. It is a challenge to her notion of personal honour and so her desire to improve herself comes head to head with her ideas about appropriateness of behaviour for girls. Leila has an internal battle.

Conventions of appropriateness

Khan's son, Mansur, finds it frustrating that he cannot meet girls. His friend introduces him to a girl who has had to become a prostitute but he finds the thought repulsive. Yet he tries to get a girl he likes into his car alone, again breaking the social rules and placing her reputation, at least, in great danger.

Tacit Theories

Mansur feels the need to be freer and persuades his reluctant father to allow him to travel with friends of his own age on a pilgrimage to Mazar-i-Sharif. This place, the location of Kalif Ali's grave, is holy for him and his fellow Muslims. He is genuinely delighted to go there, both for the freedom of travelling alone, away from his family for the first time in his life, and because of his religious fervour.

Gripped by the powerful atmosphere he decides to become a new person. He will become a new person and a pious Muslim. He will respect the hour of prayer, give alms, he will fast, go to the mosque, not look at girls before he is married, he will grow a beard, and go to Mecca. 'I am blessed,' he cries. 'I have been forgiven! I have been cleansed!' " (p. 160)

However, his resolution lasts only a week after his return.

► Commentary

The point of offering this vignette is to show that the moments of teaching and learning regimes do not just relate to teaching and learning in universities but, suitably generalised, to issues of culture more broadly. Sometimes it is easier to see how these things work when looked at in relation to a context which many readers will find unfamiliar.

► Illustrating the eight moments

The rest of the chapter explains each of the eight moments and gives examples to illustrate them. For some (for example, power relations and discursive repertoires) there is a need to spend more time elaborating the concept than for others (for example, recurrent practices). This is simply because the literature is wider and deeper in some areas and the concept more nuanced.

In offering these examples I draw extensively on the initial results of research conducted in South Africa described on p. viii. The site is not a 'typical' one of course, but is highly illuminative of change processes. Some other examples are rooted in earlier studies; especially my study with Peter Knight of 'new academics' (Knight and Trowler, 1999, 2000; Trowler and Knight, 1999, 2000), academics who are new to higher education contexts and so can see more clearly what for others has become normalised: so obvious as to become invisible to them.

Recurrent practices

As workgroups engage in tasks over time they develop ways of doing things which become 'just natural' – 'the way we do things around here'. Practices become 'hardened', normalised, and externalised through repetition, which leads to the growing feeling that 'that's the way things are'. They are taken for granted and so tend only rarely to be reflected on or evaluated. They include specific ways of using tools, such as e-mail communication, for example, and ways of behaving in meetings or with students. It is usually only new entrants to the workgroup who find these practices unusual or surprising and, after a year or so, often sink into practising them recurrently themselves. For example, one academic newly recruited from Ireland to an elite English university expressed amazement that the whole department so enthusiastically embraced the process and judgements of the Research Assessment Exercise (RAE). She recounted events at a party at which the grade achieved was revealed like a Christmas present to the staff of the department (they got a top score) and how the academics wore badges proclaiming their grade. What black hole had their critical faculties fallen into, she wondered (Trowler and Knight, 2000). For her the RAE was a flawed exercise, leading to divisions within academia and distorting the research process. Yet, in this case the very academics who should be questioning it were precisely the ones who had come not only to accept it but to celebrate it and its outcomes.

One example of 'hardening' is the use of lectures to transmit material to students. In some disciplines, in some contexts this is a recurrent practice; stereotypically in maths and physics. Yet one physicist I interviewed in South Africa challenged these practices while at the same time lamenting their widespread use in his department. He was very keen to introduce much more individual interaction among students, much more one-to-one support by lecturers, the use of workbooks and problem-based learning. He wanted students to meet problems and get stuck, and then – with support – to find a way through. He wanted students to construct knowledge about physics within their own frame of reference by fully engaging with physics problems. Here a 'Lone Ranger' in the physics department posed a head-on challenge to the established recurrent practices. He expressed the hope that his colleagues would come round to his way of thinking, but it was clear that the sets of practices being challenged were very firmly entrenched and despite his senior position in the department he would have a hard time moving out of his teaching and learning enclave. He said,

Under-prepared African students were now entering higher education in bigger classes. And the challenge was to transform our discipline to take care of that....Even 10 years since democracy the entry level of students is not that great...There were two options: to create a foundation year or to be a bit more radical and to transform the teaching of the discipline to meet the challenges [of much larger classes and under-prepared students]. We changed the teaching environment from one where the lecturer delivers the material to one where students get a chance to work through the material with a chance for group discussions afterwards....As academics in this discipline there are certain processes that go through your mind and we wanted to give students exposure to that: the thought processes in interacting with these difficult concepts.

There is nothing to lose with students getting things wrong or being stuck – engaging with the material helps them to get a handle on where the problem is, where they are stuck. Anyway we found that pass rates went up. . . . But other modules did not teach in this way unfortunately and other academics in our discipline looked at you and said 'why aren't you doing your work as a lecturer'?

Clearly, the notion of 'your work as a lecturer' involved more than all the work that this academic was doing for his students. These other academics engaged in recurrent practices of teaching which for them were simply normal, and teaching was something other than facilitating learning in the way described by this respondent. Our evaluative work at Lancaster University's Department of Educational Research has shown this sort of thing to be far from uncommon in UK universities too; in particular, HoDs instructing new staff specifically not to engage too much with teaching development but to concentrate on research and winning funding.

Tacit assumptions

All workgroups, in fact everyone, operate partly on the basis of tacit assumptions. Not to do so would simply be impracticable. Such assumptions are rarely surfaced. In fact some forms of knowing *cannot* be surfaced directly (Eraut, 2000). In teaching and learning regimes collective assumptions about, for example, assessment practices, their role and value, can influence practices in that area in very significant ways. These assumptions may have no basis in evidence, may be detrimental to good practice, and may result in practices which are more effortful and less effective than many others.

One of the characteristics of teaching and learning regimes in particular and culture in general is that reality is categorised in particular ways: there is a process of 'sorting things out' (Bowker and Star, 1999), creating dividing lines, divisions between 'this' and 'that'. Each side of these lines is assumed to be characterised in contrasting ways. One South African respondent noted that in his context academic staff believe they just 'know' what 'proper' academics are and what they are not. Thus someone with a student academic development function, a remit to improve students' academic literacy, is simply not considered a 'proper academic'. This categorisation has a number of implications for their position and power in university.

Similarly, there are sets of assumptions about the nature of 'our' discipline and the relationship it should have with the outside world. One South African HoD noted that staff in the department unquestioningly assumed that contact with industry would 'pollute' their students with uncritical and task-focused approaches, and so should be avoided. He said,

> One of the things . . . that departments like ours in this country can get split about is do we work with industry or not? . . . My sense is that we need to be a lot more like law or medicine where the profession has a positive link with us, not this view that advertisers are evil. You know, there's a wonderful Auden poem:
>
> > Thou shalt not be on friendly terms
> > with guys in advertising firms
>
> But my contact in advertising, John, is wonderfully critical, and also wonderfully generous with ideas, and I think academics can get so possessive and anal about ideas. But when I go to John we talk openly, and he gives me five good ideas and maybe I give him five good ideas.

A third example comes from law. On one campus of the newly merged South African institution a 'pure' approach was taken to legal education: students got the diet of law, and law only. On another campus students were exposed to courses on philosophy, literature, and so on. Neither questioned what they did until exposed to the other. At that point academics from the latter campus criticised the former for producing 'legal barbarians', but at the same time began to reflect on their own previously tacit assumptions about what academic law was and what its graduates should look like.

▶ Vignette: Accreditation of prior experiential learning (APEL): How tacit assumptions can become exposed to view (adapted from Trowler, 1996)

A post-1992 university decided to formalise its arrangements for the APEL. Before that each department made its own arrangements for accrediting experience outside of the academy. Many did not recognise such learning and required students to complete full degree schemes regardless of any prior experience or even in some cases other relevant qualifications. Some, however, did recognise previous experiential learning, for example, at work or through other activities. Often, though, the procedures for accrediting this were informal: basically, the admissions tutor made a decision after discussion with the candidate. In a few cases there were formal procedures for accreditation, for example, of the development of a portfolio, but these differed from department to department. The central university Registry wanted to impose some order and offer equitable treatment to all students with regard to APEL.

This initiative was essentially a rock thrown into the cultural currents of different departments in the university, exposing very different conventions of appropriateness, implicit theories, and tacit assumptions, as well as threatening the distribution of power relations in place at the time.

For some academics the process was straightforward:

> the majority of part-time students will get some accreditation for prior learning. It's very easy to do with us ... because we can easily see what they've done ... Our competencies are very clearly based around certain techniques they've got. Learning how to programme computers, for example, is something we could easily test.

> It [APEL] is ... straightforward. You can ... gauge how up-to-date the knowledge is ... you can actually categorise them quite well.

In these cases the straightforward 'skills and knowledge' theory of teaching and learning was in place: knowledge is seen as a measurable and concrete property which can be acquired in any context and is easily measured and accredited. For other academics, though, the APEL process was not so straightforward:

> We are reluctant [to get involved in APEL] ... most people in the beginning of the course have views on [the discipline] which are over-simplistic so most people's prior experience if anything wouldn't be that relevant ... [the area of study] requires understanding of ... [discipline X and discipline Y] and familiarity with the literature.

Another, commenting on a student who appeared to have relevant experience, said that

> Well that still doesn't mean [he] can hack academic work, academic discipline.

A third explained why her colleagues rejected the idea:

> There is a terrific sense of elitism about the subject, a terrific amount of almost snobbery about it.

Academics like these tend to defend the battlements of their areas of study against attacks upon them (Barnett, 1990, 1994) with the traditional weapons of the 'the essay' and 'the literature'. Higher education is much more than of the acquisition of knowledge, conceptualised as a commodity. While the higher education curriculum is undoubtedly undergoing a shift in the relationship between thought and action so that what counts as knowing is increasingly adopting an operational character (Barnett, 1994, p. 48), this has by no means expressed itself within teaching and learning regimes in every context.

▶ **Commentary**

This vignette shows, then, that an initiative like APEL can disturb previously subterranean conflicts or differences within teaching and learning regimes, and can expose the character of these potentially conflicting differences. It is only when there is a forced engagement with a contentious issue that tacit assumptions, power relations, conventions of appropriateness, and so on become 'visible'. Such a process can be beneficial to a department or workgroup which wishes to reflect on its ways of doing things.

Implicit theories of teaching and learning

These are integral to many of the tacit assumptions found within workgroups. Implicit theories are different from assumptions in that they are more elaborate when unpacked and are more focused on the detailed processes of learning and teaching. They underpin practices in that area.

Implicit theories encompass theories about teaching and learning – constructivist versus transmissive, for example – which come to inform practice. Constructivist learning theory, which suggests that learning involves incorporating new knowledge into pre-existing cognitive frameworks, also involves theories about knowledge and knowing. Rarely discussed or made explicit (outside of teacher education courses), such tacit theories shape notions of 'good practice'. Transmissive learning theory has very different understandings of the nature of knowledge and knowing, and about how learning takes place. Such theories may also include theories about students and their abilities, the curriculum, disadvantage, and equity. Implicit theories are more likely to be surfaced from time to time than tacit assumptions are, partly because they relate to practice in a more direct way, and partly simply because they are closer to formal academic knowledge and so there is more likelihood that at least in part they will be made explicit.

There was a clear division among my South African respondents between those who believed in innate student ability, which was more or less immutable, and those who believed that student performance was heavily conditioned by their background and was malleable. Clearly, in South Africa there are still huge divisions between advantaged and disadvantaged students. These two implicit theories about the nature of student ability each have very contrasting implications for practice: should students be left to essentially sink or swim in the higher education context (those with natural ability will, after all, survive; those without would fail anyway); should there be very strong provision of student support to counteract disadvantage; or should there be much more radical changes to the higher education curriculum and practices to make it a more hospitable environment for disadvantaged students who come with different types of cultural capital?

One of my respondents gave a specific illustration of how practices changed when implicit theories about these issues were challenged. He said,

> We had a member of staff, a theoretician, who, when he came here said – 'Standards are the key thing – we should select our students and leave them to sink or swim. I'm the only person around here who's maintaining standards and I shall maintain standards.' He came from an American situation and had to have the difficulties of certain groups of students in South Africa pointed out to him. Once he realised this he changed his position . . . . We looked through our materials, our workbooks. We found examples about the . . . . walls of an igloo. Many of our black students didn't know what an igloo was! We even got to the point of talking about the processes in a photographic plate in a camera. We eradicated these culturally-based examples – has there been a transformation in teaching our discipline? Decidedly, yes.

These implicit theories are not always generated wholly or mainly within the workgroup. They may come from pre-service or in-service training courses or may result from disciplinary socialisation. Whatever their origin, their impact on the practices of the workgroup is nonetheless significant. Thus a transmissive theory of learning may guide the architect's thinking about the design of teaching spaces in universities: a lectern, perhaps, with rows of tiered seating facing it; or the design of a clear 'front' to the room where attention is directed. Such designs are predicated on the idea of the expert who transmits his/her knowledge to a group of students.

A transmissive theory, and the provision of a room based on it, will condition the lecturer's planning of sessions and their conduct of them, so that the lecture mode predominates and little space is created for students to play with and use ideas, to practice new language, to apply and synthesise knowledge, or to explore the impact of new ideas upon old learning.

► **Vignette: The Reinvention Centre at Warwick University**

'Warwick and Brookes Win £3.3 Million to Reinvent Undergraduate Education', runs the headline on a Warwick University web page (Warwick, 2007a). The £3.3 million amount seems a fairly modest sum for such a lofty ambition. The Reinvention Centre at Westwood, Warwick, was designed and built as part of this larger reinvention project. The space is designed to be flexible enough so as not to 'reduce teaching to preordained formats'. The furniture can be moved around and takes the form of large cubes, benches, and a chaise longue. There are no desks. The floor is a heated, rubberised surface so that no furniture is actually necessary for sitting, lying or working. The shape and purpose of the space can be transformed. For a while there was deliberately no 'front' – though demand from academics and their students for a fixed digital projector and screen imposed this on the room to some extent.

The room is designed to encourage interaction between teacher and students and to facilitate research-based learning. The design aims for 'an atmosphere of creativity and innovation'. So, underpinning the design there is a theory of teaching and learning, quite an explicit one in this case, based on constructivist and progressivist thinking.

The following are some relevant website (Warwick, 2007b) quotes from students who have used the room:

Promotes active learning
Breaks boundaries
Not the usual boring teaching room
Allows very unstructured lessons
First steps towards something big!
I like the space and the informal layout
Challenge to the way we think, research and learn
Much more relaxed and allows us to be more open
Spacious– allows for moving around and interacting
Not formal class structure: no chairs, tables, board

Good place to interact and have active discussions
Warm/relaxed/social working environment
Makes you realise you can think outside the box
Maybe slightly more comfortable seating
Encourages both students and learners to think outside the
    box ... it promotes freedom of speech and thinking
Different; not formal – spacious and freethinking, suggests lots
    of room for ideas and innovation
It is different from any type of learning I have experienced
    at university – a nice change!
Easily rearranged for different types of work, e.g. lecture, presen-
    tation, group work

▶ Commentary

The reinvention project, and this space, seeks to challenge what is seen as the unhelpful tacit theories and implicit assumptions built into university spaces, and to change teaching and learning practices through examples. 'Reinvention', though, is quite a difficult thing to do: the past pulls like an elastic band and the present imposes itself very strongly. The Reinvention Centre at Westwood tackles the issue of space, yet it is set in a peripheral part of the main Warwick campus and is situated in a cul-de-sac at the end of another cul-de-sac found only by entering the first cul-de-sac. Space design issues at this more macro level say as much about the Centre and tradition as the Centre itself does about traditional teaching and learning. The comments from the students are inadvertently illustrative of the problems associated with 'reinvention' too. The use of the word 'lessons' by one student indicates the legacy of school in that person's thinking. And the contrast between the experience of learning at the Centre and their usual practices hints that this is for these students a refreshing, but rather special, place that in no way touches their higher education experience more broadly. Moreover, there are students that we don't hear from, and in particular those in the hard sciences who have not yet been introduced to the space. So far (September 2007) its use has been largely limited to creative arts and social science and humanities disciplines. Academics elsewhere have not chosen to take advantage of it.

Discursive repertoires

'Discourse' is a term with multiple meanings (see Grant *et al*., 1998, for a summary). Here the word is used to mean language as social practice, as produced in recurrent ways that are conditioned by social structures. Discourse is both inclusive and exclusive in its effect, setting up a range of options and exclusions:

> Textuality itself is composed not just of what is said or written but also by what is left aside, unsaid, in choosing this signifier or that image to construct a particular meaning. Therefore to deconstruct discourses is to examine not only the textual presences but also those absences implied by the present terms; that is, to read beyond and thus foreground the unsaid and the unsayable within texts.
>
> (Fenwick, 2004, pp. 174–175)

Discursive repertoires, one aspect of discourse, involve the production of pieces of text (orally, in writing, in graphical form, or in physical objects) recurrently applied in social settings. The repertoire may include words, phrases, or other components of text: a set of resources which individuals and groups use. Such repertoires provide a kind of shorthand but at the same time structure and limit the range of expression. The way they both limit and enable thought and actions structures the way projects and tasks are conceived, discussed, and pursued. Like discourse itself, the character of these repertoires is linked to social structures: to ideologies; to cultures; and to other broader dimensions of social life which render practices regular.

Discursive repertoires link to the other moments in organic ways – for example, they appeal to particular codes of signification and can reinforce or challenge existing patterns of power relations. Many writers have noted the relationship between discourse and power. Indeed, *Language and Power* is the title of one of Fairclough's classic texts in the field (1989). The discursive turn in social science highlights the fact that oral written or iconic texts produced by organisational members are intimately connected to issues of power relationships, effectiveness, or control (Cooren, 2004, p. 374). So, like each of the other moments of teaching and learning regimes, this one cannot really be separated out from the others, and is only treated distinctly here for the purpose of clarity.

For Bakhtin, language is intimately related to social context. While discourse reflects social structures such as ideologies it is also intimately impregnated with the sediment of history and context. He writes,

> There are no 'neutral' words and forms – words and forms that can belong to 'no one'; language has been completely taken over, shot through with intentions and accents. For any individual consciousness living in it, language is not an abstract system of normative forms but

rather a concrete heteroglot conception of the world. All words have the 'taste' of a profession, the genre, a tendency, a party, a particular work, a particular person, a generation, an age group, the day and hour. Each word tastes of the context and context in which it has lived its socially charged life; all words and forms are populated by intentions.

(Bakhtin, 1981, p. 293)

We can see something of that, perhaps, in the student's use of the word 'lessons' in the vignette above.

Within workgroups in universities discursive repertoires flow in from broader social structures and are developed and used locally too, giving a local flavour and a particular way of seeing and describing the world. However, this is not necessarily only a natural, organic process, but the natural outcome of social processes. Discursive repertoires can be manufactured, deliberately manipulated as a management tool as one of the levers of culture. This happens, apparently, at Disneyland, which also has its own 'university':

Language is a central feature of university life, and new employees are schooled in its proper use. Customers at Disneyland... are never referred to as such; they are 'guests'. There are no rides at Disneyland, only 'attractions'... Law enforcement personnel hired by the park are not policemen but 'security hosts'... And of course there are no accidents at Disneyland, only *'incidents'*.

(Van Maanen and Kunda, 1989, p. 63)

Even such obviously inauthentic practices may work their way into the cultural life of organisations, making the distinction between 'authentic' and 'inauthentic' hard to draw:

Many members use the terms super and terrific in enthusiastic tones after relatively banal statements, a custom that seems to have worked its way down the hierarchy. The use of over-worked cliches in earnest ways also suggests a merging of the individual with the organization.

(Van Maanen and Kunda, 1989, p. 81)

Prichard (2000) has addressed this issue. He attempts to distinguish, on the one hand, the structural forces which condition practices, perspectives, and priorities, and the power of individuals to challenge them, on the other. He quotes one of his respondents who considers herself 'forced' to be a particular kind of higher education manager, concerned with efficiency, economies, and balancing the budget. He asks where this force comes from:

> It is 'done', I have argued, through the distributed discursive practices of audits, planning and budgets. Within these there are verbal/symbolic processes which position [people] within the 'paper structure' of charts, budgets, and spreadsheets. These are embodied, spatially and physically, in the new vertically integrated management teams and in the one-to-one audits and performance appraisal processes.
>
> (Prichard, 2000, p. 153)

These 'distributed discursive practices' form part of what he calls the managerial station, an imposed social order with associated discursive practices. But, as well as the managerial station with its distinctive discourse attempting to colonise identities and practices, there are more agentic 'locales'. These are established and maintained at the grassroots, developed as part of dealing with the lived realities there: particular histories, contexts, issues, and sets of interactions. Stations and locales coexist in a situation of tension and struggle, so that in the case above the individual manager is able to recognise and resist the forces upon her. She is able to recognise the ways in which the preferred practices and outlook of the managerial station reduce the quality of life, contravene her principles, and work to position her subjectivity in ways which contradict her wishes. Domination, resistance, and struggle involve discourse as well as other kinds of practices.

The discursive repertoires found in teaching and learning regimes are, then, often multiple, contested, and in contest. Usually no one discourse is fully established, it is only one among many competing discourses, though one or more, that may be dominant, hegemonic. Alternative ways of being, alternative identities, and alternative sets of meaning are associated with competing discourses, so that the issue is not simply a linguistic one, and outcomes of discursive contest constitute alternative ways of being in the world. The vignette on pp. 139–141 illustrates this point, as does the one immediately below.

▶ Vignette: The 'new route' PhD at Hilltop University (adapted from Trowler and Knight, 2001)

The vice chancellor of Hilltop University was on good personal terms with a nationally known and respected figure in HE policy development,

Professor Prozelytiser. At a break during a meeting in London they discussed the latter's enthusiasm for a 'new route' to the PhD in the United Kingdom: Prozelytiser's vision of an 'enhanced' PhD.

Prozelytiser's view was that the traditional British PhD is too narrow and too focused on research rather than the needs of the economy and the career needs of PhD students. As a result the overseas PhD market was increasingly being lost to North America, where, Prozelytiser argued, taught doctorates provided the breadth and requisite skills for the needs of both the economy and the individual.

> The consequences for British interests and for the UK's share of the overseas student market [of a drain of PhD students to the USA] should not be under estimated . . . Some [of the provision which underpins British PhDs at the moment are] spatchcock taught elements into PhD programmes on an ad hoc basis for individual students. Sponsors are scornful of this amateur approach . . . The developmental elements will be in pulling this all together within the participating universities and overcoming the considerable conservatism that exists in some subject areas . . . . [so that provision is of the same order as] in the USA, which is the competition we are seeking to excel.
>
> (Prozelytizer, 2000, p. 2)

Some time later Professor Prozelytiser won funding to put his proposal into practice. A consortium of universities was assembled. The 'new route' would be designed to offer 'what the sponsors want', an American-style PhD, yet one which is better than those available in the United States. It was hoped that the new taught programme would enable the students to develop a range of capacities including communication skills, information technology, enterprise skills, technology transfer, the formation of spin-out companies, and business methods.

At Hilltop University there was little or no consultation or even awareness of this development until the new dean for postgraduate studies received a message from the vice chancellor telling him to ensure that Hilltop was fully involved in the new scheme. Soon the 'new route' proposal was put to the directors of doctoral programmes in an individual process of 'tell and sell'. One of these, the Director of the Doctoral Programme in Implementation Studies, circulated details of the 'new route' proposal to colleagues involved in that programme: the 'doctoral workgroup'.

Their responses were mixed: from cautious to negative through to hostile. They raised issues about the practicality of the proposal and about resource implications. More important, though, was their reaction to the discursive repertoires used by Professor Prozelytiser. One of the individuals in the workgroup reacted strongly to them: 'I find some of the language in the document offensive.' They saw this discourse as an instance of the managerialist discourse of new higher education (NHE): a discourse which portrays knowledge as a commodity to be bought and sold; higher education as a service industry for the economy; students as receptacles of skills; and lecturers as simply 'deliverers' of the curriculum (Trowler, 2001). Increasingly prevalent in higher education, NHE discourse draws on the language of finance ('franchising', 'credit accumulation') and of industry ('product delivery', 'line management', 'customers'). It contrasts sharply with the traditional discourse of higher education which had quite different ideological roots. Publicly available materials about the doctoral programme in implementation studies were framed in this discourse:

> The aim of the programme is to provide an opportunity for experienced professionals to become autonomous researchers and to gain deeper and more critical insight into their own professional practices and concerns. This is a single aim, since the programme is designed to review and reinforce the linkages between research as a method of knowledge acquisition and as a vehicle for the rearticulation and negotiation of professional concerns.

From the perspective of the doctoral workgroup, then, the discursive repertoires employed were rooted in a managerialist ideology which they found repugnant: it was this ideology rather than the language itself which they were objecting to.

Needless to say, the new route was not adopted as a structure for the Doctoral Programme in Implementation Studies.

► Commentary

This vignette demonstrates the significance of discursive repertoires in policy development, in particular their relationship to those which already exist on the ground. Where there is congruence there is more likely to be successful implementation. But where, as here, the discursive repertoires employed are neither salient nor congruent to those in the context described then they are likely to impede rather than facilitate change. Discursive repertoires are intimately related to ideologies, a very significant structural feature which conditions behaviour, including the production of text. One of the questions which educational ideologies relate to is 'what is higher education actually for?' An enterprise ideology (see Endnote) responds in terms of vocational preparation, whereas a traditionalist ideology responds in terms of disciplinary training. The clashing discursive repertoires displayed here were rooted in these contrasting ideological positions.

▶ Vignette: Contesting discourses in higher education curriculum (adapted from Moore, 2003)

Two competing discourses about the nature and structure of higher education are found in the South African context. One, the disciplinary discourse, refers to 'the traditional currency of courses and qualifications, based on longstanding academic propositions about the need for sequential learning within defined disciplines' (Ensor, 2004, p. 342). The other is the credit exchange discourse, based on the modular programmes and the accumulation of credits with students able to choose modules and construct their own programmes of study in a flexible way, allowing for the more seamless interface between work and study.

The credit exchange discourse is found in many South African policy documents. In particular, its National Qualifications Framework (NQF) is based on this discourse, recommending the organisation of higher education by programmes rather than departments. It is propagated by senior figures in higher education system there who draw on the work of Scott (1995) and Gibbons et al. (1994) to provide a rationale for this model of higher education. Those writers were invited to South Africa to discuss their ideas and helped to provide the model adopted there.

The argument underpinning the credit exchange discourse is that globalisation and the needs of developing and developed economies require a more 'up-to-date' structure of higher education. How true that argument is need not detain us here: the point is that the credit exchange discourse and curricular model was being promoted in South Africa as a preferred model which should replace the earlier disciplinary model and the discourse associated with it.

The credit exchange model became enshrined in the South African NQF, which aimed to reshape and rationalise the qualifications system in that country. A change process was put in place to implement the framework. The main elements of this change involved a move towards a modular curriculum and the reshaping of universities to become closer to a mode II formation (Gibbons et al., 1994): one which addressed problems rather than disciplinary issues, which was flexible, which involved both universities and industry, and which was essentially temporary so that as problems were solved organisational structures dissolved. The intention was that the dominant, mode I, formations would wither away.

The problem for the influential academics and policy makers who were promoting the credit exchange model and discourse was that most faculties of science and humanities in South Africa were, and continued to be, orientated around the disciplinary discourse. The curricular implications of this were to organise modules or courses into coherent pathways, linear in nature, with the aim of inducting students into a discipline in a kind of apprenticeship. The attempt to impose a credit exchange model and its discourse within institutions was accompanied by different levels of anxiety and turmoil (Moore, 2002). Where attempts were made to reorganise the undergraduate curriculum wholesale along credit exchange lines there was great antagonism from academics. Battle lines were drawn and conflict broke out between those determined to hang on to the disciplinary discourse and the ideology underpinning it on the one hand, and those determined to implement a credit exchange curriculum and a different discourse and ideology on the other; the details of these battles are spelled out in Ensor (2001, 2004) and Moore (2002).

Moore (2003) offers two case studies of this conflict, both being universities in South Africa (UniA and UniB).

While in both contexts we have seen academics respond negatively to the policy, resentful at their loss of autonomy, at the challenge to well-established roles and identities, and at the escalation of their administrative loads, these were features of the UniA context mostly at the start of the programmatisation process, and by early 2000, these resentments seem to have been replaced by a general acceptance of, in some quarters even enthusiasm for, the new arrangements. At UniB, by contrast, protests, challenges and conflict have been much more persistent, and some of the programme constructs have been much more unstable as a consequence (Moore, 2003, p. 135).

Moore uses the example of the programme called Development Studies and Social Transformation in UniB. He quotes one of his respondents discussing the tensions around developing this programme in line with the credit exchange discourse:

> Okay, so instead of having a [single] carefully constructed notion of Development Theory, [the] course called Cities of the South ... has a whole lot of human geography theory about where cities come from and so on. [Politics] has got a course in Development Management which has its own set of theories. Anthropology has got another one. Sociology has got something called Introduction to Development Theory .... and then there was a very interesting argument about a

discipline which said 'In other disciplines we don't treat theory in the same kind of way as you do'.... We have to accept the notion that we treat theory in different kinds of ways.... We had a situation where people were saying we're not going to offer anything new, we're just going to take the existing courses and shove them in... and [they] will pretend that they fit together, but they didn't. There was no way that they were designed together. In fact, we had quite a strong argument from people here who were saying 'we don't have time to make and fit together. We refuse to have meetings, or even to circulate course outlines to each other to see what each other is doing'. There was that level of recalcitrance and disillusionment.

(Moore, 2003, p. 136)

▶ **Commentary**

This vignette again illustrates two competing discourses. They had always been present, differing, for example, on the nature of 'graduateness'. In this case, though, one stresses the continuing significance of disciplines, the other the necessity for curriculum restructuring. Underpinning this narrative is an ideological dispute between *traditionalism* and its disciplinary discourse on the one hand and the *enterprise* ideology, with elements of *social reconstructionism*, which both emphasise in different ways the socio-economic mission of higher education, on the other.

Some strands of sociocultural theory, for example, Wenger (1998), emphasise the development of discourse communities characterised by intersubjectivity and by mutually understood ways of interpreting and producing text. Members of these so-called 'interpretive communities' (Fish, 1980) have no difficulty in understanding each other and will usually understand a text presented to them in roughly the same way as each other. While this description is very dubious (and Fish's work has been heavily criticised), what is clear is that as workgroups engage together over long periods of time on common projects they do develop distinctive ways of talking, writing, and interpreting text. These are not the only discursive resources available to them, but they represent a broadening of the options available for discursive production.

Meanwhile, disciplines have their own particular discourses, and within them contextually specific sub-discourses (Winberg, 2003). The study of the disciplinary discourses has tended to concentrate on written forms of discourse, perhaps because it is easier to research, and because the study of academic conventions is an important area of preparation for students and has a functional role in universities.

One example of academic discursive genres is given by Berkenkotter and Huckin (1995), who show how the structure and content of scientific articles has changed over the course of a century to become more like those of newspaper articles. This discursive change is intimately linked to changes in social practice – particularly the faster pace of academic life, the information revolution, and the consequent need that scientists have to fillet, select, and absorb key aspects of information very quickly. Thus the use of abstracts has become universal over that period, and key findings are presented earlier in the paper with less attention being given to descriptions of methodology or other content which is secondary to the central information being imparted.

Despite such broad trends, the localisation of discourse also involves unique connotations. Words and phrases are used (or not used) in particular ways with localised meanings. What happens is that the generic form is locally 'accented', a locally situated dialect develops dynamically but is not widely shared. The *particular* characteristics of activity locally provide space for diversity and agency in discourse.

So, for example, Winberg (2003) shows how the language of academic architecture involves a number of discursive genres: the language of construction and the language of design, for example. There are rules about how texts should be written or spoken, and these differ according to the discursive mode – a site report, a pitch to a client, a design specification. Successful students must become literate in these different discursive genres. The sites and contexts for their acquisition tend to differ: the language of construction in workshops and on site, for example, or the design specification in the classroom. Thus discourse and context are linked. Students learn to talk like an architect in context-appropriate ways and they learn to do this in design-studio spaces as well as on site and in the lecture theatre. Both structure (the discursive forms available) and agency (the choices made about their use in particular contexts) are at work here.

In the South African context I found that the backstories, the narratives that groups shared about their history and the broader context, were extremely important discursively. There was a cast of characters about whom views were shared and disputed, a series of events which were positioned as being of significance for the present day, and a set of issues which were wrangled over and which impinged on current discussions in important ways. This backstory mediated and made contextually specific the discursive characteristics associated with the discipline, although these remained strong.

One group I studied there revealed a common set of discursive resources which was shared in a very distinctive way. Built up over a period of years, and to some extent self-selecting, the members of this group were all steeped in constructivist educational theory. They had read many of the key texts, discussed the ideas, and attempted to apply them in the science degree foundation course they designed and delivered. Their production of text in the focus group interview was littered with metaphors, references, and vocabulary derived from this literature and ways of thinking about education. This had little, if anything, to do with the scientific disciplines in which the members of this group were socialised, but rather was a product of the group itself. A very clear discursive community was in place here. The next vignette is about them.

▶ Vignette: A consensual teaching and learning regime in South Africa

A pre-degree undergraduate access teaching group were intensely concerned about maintaining the quality of their teaching in the face of reduced resources but increased student numbers in their new, merged South African institution.

They could see their previously generous resource base coming down to the levels found elsewhere among the other parts of the newly merged institution. They also felt that their very successful approach to preparing students for undergraduate study was not acknowledged at all by the management of the merged institution.

This [pre-degree] programme has been acknowledged as the best in the country, delivered by a successful cohesive unit that has done incredibly well... We've had ten years of experience on this programme but now there is no acknowledgement of our past success [by the hierarchy]... It's a real slap in the face. We've worked so hard for so long to build the programme ....

They saw themselves, and the campus in which they worked, as different – and more successful – than other parts of the new institution:

There are certain cultural differences at our campus in the way we operate – in our teaching and our management – compared to the other campuses. We want to hang on to what we've enjoyed, especially as we can't see anything better.... Change is very difficult and we are no strangers to change. This programme has evolved since the moment it started, but we can't see anything in prospect that we can relate to. It's very disheartening.

The special, successful, practices which they had developed over time were based on a philosophy which was quite explicit and shared by the group: they each made many references to it during the discussion:

> Our teaching philosophy has been very well thought out and we keep very up to date with the literature, using ideas in the literature in our practice.... The culture of our campus has been to have a well thought-out teaching philosophy with a good base in the literature. We have been encouraged to do that as the base to our programme. Other campuses have never had a [pre-degree] course from the beginning and don't have that approach to their practice.

All members of the group contributed to an answer when I asked them to make the characteristics of their philosophy explicit, though in fact they mainly described their teaching and learning practices rather than the philosophical underpinning to them.

They were able to articulate their philosophy and practices very quickly, very collaboratively, and in a mutually confirming way. They quoted the work of John Biggs, referred to the deep and surface learning literature, and described themselves as constructivist in their approach. In relation to practices, one said,

> Our approach is materials-driven, it's student-centred with interaction being really important so we need low staff–student ratios. We engage students in small group work: it's experiential, mediated learning. It's not chalk and talk.

However, this had already come under threat:

> I've already found myself having to resort to chalk and talk... When you have very large numbers you have to dictate to some extent. The students are [no longer] learning by their mistakes. You can't afford for them to make mistakes because there are just too many of them. You really can't do it another way unless you are prepared for the whole experience to go out of the window. This goes against the kind of teaching we believe in. It's not just fitting people for jobs, it's fitting people to create their own jobs.

Yet they still retained their group identity and wanted very much to resist any developments which would have deleterious consequences for students:

I think we are very much together. We've got a strong emphasis on sharing: there's no feeling of concealing knowledge or protecting knowledge. We aren't interested in – what's it called? – yes, intellectual property. That's so destructive. There's a lot of emphasis on teamwork and co-operative learning which we are modelling as staff.

But now we're now asked to make compromises which would mean that we might as well pack up and go home – because we would have to throw out the philosophy. And throw out the successful practices based on it: it's a complete waste of time, what they want us to do. It's hard enough trying to do a good job, let alone having to defend yourself and justify what you do. There's no space to be heard because of the hierarchies, it's just 'Shut up. Get on with it.' We aren't used to that: our Faculty in this campus before the merger was extremely supportive. But the new hierarchy has never actually asked us what our philosophy was: you are not allowed to say that you are the best practice model. They are missing an opportunity for something really positive to happen, for investing in people, for developing people.

It appeared that the group had been carefully 'built' as well as developing organically. There had been a degree of self-selection into the group over the years, and the leader had been in place from the beginning and so had been able to shape the group through careful choices and a consistent strategy. They very clearly shared what I have called elsewhere a progressivist educational ideology (Trowler, 1998, p. 70). Perhaps significantly, all those members of the group that I talked to were women, and all except one were white (though the lone black woman said nothing until encouraged to so by the group's leader).

▶ **Commentary**

Arguably here was a community of practice as classically articulated by Wenger:

[Communities of practice are characterised by . . .].
  1) sustained mutual relationships – harmonious or conflictual
  2) shared ways of engaging in doing things together
  3) the rapid flow of information and propagation of innovation
  4) absence of introductory preambles, as if conversations and interactions were merely the continuation of an ongoing process
  5) very quick setup of a problem to be discussed

6) substantial overlap in participants' descriptions of who belongs
7) knowing what others know, what they can do, and how they can contribute to an enterprise
8) mutually defining identities
9) the ability to assess the appropriateness of actions and products
10) specific tools, representations, and other artifacts
11) local lore, shared stories, inside jokes, knowing laughter
12) jargon and short cuts to communication as well as the ease of producing new ones
13) certain styles recognized as displaying membership
14) a shared discourse reflecting a certain perspective on the world
(Wenger, 1998, 125–126)

Wenger's description of how such a community 'makes the job possible' (see p. 30) certainly seems to be happening in this example. However, this highly functional group had a number of advantages which helped them develop this distinctive consensus. Among these were the following: the group had been built in a deliberative way over a number of years; members were self-selecting and had many characteristics in common (they were all women around the same age, for example); there was a leader with a clear sense of purpose; the members were all motivated by a coherent and shared set of values around the issue of widening participation.

The commonality exemplified in this vignette, this level of consensus in terms of discourse, is perhaps unusual. Often there are multiple, alternative, sometimes competing discourses in operation. So, for example, this South African HoD draws on managerialist discourse, probably in unhelpful ways, in dealing with the common curriculum issue:

In my opinion there was a very poor academic standard [on campus X]. The people who were running this were competent in teaching and nothing very much else. When we came to take over . . . the first thing I did was to try and streamline undergraduate studies. Coming together with campus X gave us the opportunity to re-write and regularise what they were doing . . . We had to increase the number of credits for each course because the administration had been hugely out of proportion to the learning outcomes [on small credit courses] . . . It was a nightmare.

We left the most difficult characters out of the negotiations: We decided early on that this really wasn't an ideological battle and I didn't have the time or patience or energy to take those people with me.

Now that we are actually doing it we are finding that it's not easy. On paper it was a lot easier. What we're finding now is that that high-point of co-operation is something really of the past. One of the people who was involved is now out of the equation – she was a fantastically good planner and clear strategic thinker. So even though she didn't know too much about the area, some areas, she had very good structural vision . . . . And the people that we are left with are a lot more . . . prepared to argue over everything. What we are concerned with now is the lack of communication . . . They don't answer our letters . . . . In our planning document we have common outcomes but we don't have a common grading system and have to try to agree on one.

Discursive use is a site of tension. There are structural forces which tend to homogenise and unify discursive use and agentic, local, situated processes which lend diversity to it. Discursive forms are therefore both generic and local, both reproduced (enacted) and constituted (constructed). The reproduction of genres occurs when recurrent behaviours involve comparable situations with comparable discursive responses – the tradition wields a power of its own. Berger and Luckmann (1966) and Schutz and Luckmann (1989) characterise the individual saying to themselves effectively, 'here we go again', as recurrent practices and associated discursive forms begin to solidify into social structures. Discursive practices become 'just normal'.

What recurs is not a material situation . . . but our construal of a type. The typified situation, including typifications of participants, underlies typification in rhetoric. Successful communication would require that participants share common types; this is possible insofar as types are socially created.

(Schutz and Luckmann, 1989, pp. 156–157)

Bergvall (1992, p. 1) writes,

Academic discourse takes place on a variety of levels: casual hallway chats, lectures, conversations between teachers and students in and out of class, e-mail, memos, scholarly papers, books. Each of these is a form of academic 'conversation', with a variety of levels of formality, personal involvement, number of participants, etc . . . . Usually conversation is a natural pattern learned in childhood, but the appropriate use of voice in academic conversation, particularly the monologic style, requires extensive training, and enculturation into the modes of conversation sanctioned by academic discourse communities. New members must learn style, vocabulary, citation format, organization and length of texts or talk

This socialisation into 'appropriate' discourses happens in a number of ways:

> Given the chance to observe and practice in situ the behaviour of members of a culture, people pick up the relevant jargon, imitate behaviour, and gradually start to act in accordance with its norms. These cultural practices are often recondite and extremely complex. Nevertheless, given the opportunity to observe and practice them, people adopt them with great success. Students, for instance, can quickly get an implicit sense of what is suitable diction, what makes a relevant question, what is legitimate or illegitimate behaviour in a particular activity
>
> (Brown *et al.*, 1989, p. 34)

Increasingly, these conventions are being made explicit in 'how to' style books for novice researchers and students, rather than relying on their simply being 'picked up' over time. Induction into the 'discourse community' (insofar as one exists) may therefore become more ordered. However, it is more difficult to do this in relation to the 'conversations of the discipline' (Bazerman, 1994) – the issues that are the subject of debate within a discipline or sub-discipline. These are dynamic, localised, and often specific to specialities within disciplines.

▶ Vignette: Discursive struggle in South Africa

In the South African context the conflict between the discourse of 'transformation' (addressing the structural inequalities which are the legacy of apartheid) and the discourse of quality, each with their associated discursive repertoires, forms another example of discourse as a site of tension and struggle.

One respondent in the South African study, the physicist quoted earlier (p. 68), commented on his attempts to bring about a student-centred curriculum in the face of opposition from colleagues and others who were ostensibly concerned about quality:

> When you are making a change like this in a traditional environment you find many sceptics, especially when it involves getting off your

behind and doing more work [in preparing workbooks and seeing students in one-one sessions]. Then many people try to find reasons why it should not be done: there are accusations of coaching the students and that sort of thing. You have got your colleagues against you. The problem was that they would have to re-think what they were doing...We still haven't succeeded in that though: within the school of physics teaching remains largely traditional and colleagues at [one of the previously independent institutions before the merger] have not been exposed to this approach. Physicists are largely conservative in their approach, but with recurriculation [in terms of what we teach and how we teach it] the age of modernism is coming in and some people are catching up. The refusal to bring on modernism is now being questioned....But approaches are people-dependent: these new approaches involve caring for people, and you cannot imbue caring. What's nice about the merger is that it has given us the chance to reflect on what we do....I think the change at the moment is good – it's got lots of positives towards the future. I mentioned the antagonism of colleagues, but what I find is that as the movement grows, if you are able to ride the tide, people may not do exactly what you are doing and they won't acknowledge your influence but they feel they have to start thinking a little bit more about what they are doing: they start to feel that all is not so well and that they cannot stay in their comfort zone....You won't get 100% conversion, and besides I don't think you want 100% conversion because you don't want to settle from one comfort zone into another comfort zone.

► **Commentary**

The following points are worth noticing here:

1. The underpinning ideology being drawn on here situates students' performance as a function of the opportunities available to them prior to entering higher education: they are not bright or weak; rather they are better prepared or under-prepared for study. This is an anti-essentialist ideology: there is nothing immutable about the potential of individual students. This is reflected in the choices made in drawing on discursive repertoires: 'under-prepared' rather than 'lower quality' or 'less qualified'.

2. Similarly, the experiences offered within higher education are very significant in terms of outcomes: changing teaching approaches can have real effects on student performance even in challenging

circumstances. Thus the respondent refers to the 'entry level of students' rather than 'standard of students', the clear implication being that prior disadvantage can be overcome.

3. The alternative location of colleagues is depicted in terms of the discourse of derision: they are largely lazy (not getting 'off their behinds'), uncaring traditionalists, in a 'comfort zone', refusing to accept the inevitability of 'modernism'.

4. Change is viewed positively: it provides a chance to reflect and see the error of old ways, realising that 'all is not so well'. Eventually more and more will change their practices as the inevitability of the need for change in new circumstances hits them.

Although I did not interview any of this respondent's colleagues, apparently much more influenced than him by the traditionalist educational ideology, they clearly would have been drawing on an alternative set of discursive repertoires, being more likely to use words like 'quality', 'standards', and 'deterioration' rather than 'modernism'. We hear through this respondent that the traditionalist position involves scepticism in relation to his student-centred approach, viewing it as 'coaching' (interpreted in terms of hand-holding, mollycoddling). They would be much less likely to take a positive view of change and to see it as threatening.

A final point is that in the United Kingdom, the discourse of student-centredness and that of quality have been brought together via the mediating discourse of 'the student experience'. Whether this represents resolution or co-option is for the reader to judge.

Conventions of appropriateness

Associated with several of the other moments described above, conventions of appropriateness are understandings developed over time about the kinds of behaviours associated with teaching and learning which are, and are not, appropriate. These include how an academic behaves in the classroom; the kinds of interactions he or she has with students; whether and how textbooks are used; what students are expected to do; the extent to which they engage in an active way; where the focus of attention is. Conventions of appropriateness developed in a TLR condition what feels normal and what feels deviant in relation to teaching, learning, and assessment. They are often codified in, for example, student handbooks.

We rarely recognise the extent to which our conscious estimates of what is worthwhile and what is not are due to standards of which we are

not conscious at all. But in general it may be said that the things which
we take for granted without inquiry or reflection are just the things
which determine our conscious thinking and decide our conclusions.
And these habitudes which lie below the level of reflection are just those
which have been formed in the constant give and take of relationship
with others.

(Dewey, 1916, p. 22)

▶ Vignette: Conventions of Appropriateness in Academic Publishing

Conventions of appropriateness are most easily seen in their transgression. They are most visible too when they concern written conventions.
Two case studies involving the transgression of written conventions in
research are offered by Berkenkotter and Huckin (1995). In the first,
a biologist, June Davis, attempts to publish her findings in the respected
journal *Infection and Immunity*. She is unwilling, however, to situate her
results within a 'phony story' involving a larger tradition of research, wish-
ing instead to highlight the original features of her findings. The problem
is that the editor and reviewers insist that she situate the findings within
a series of citations of other work, thus changing her narrative from a
local one highlighting her findings within the tradition of her own work
to one which involves work of a wider segment of the scientific community. Finally, she has to acquiesce if she wishes to see her work published,
and so the 'phony story' is constructed.

A second example offered by Berkenkotter and Huckin relates to
the attempt to set up a journal in the area of modern languages,
one which was more responsive to readers and explored new ways of
communicating with them. *The Reader of Literature: a newsletter of
reader-oriented criticism and teaching* would be a forum for readers,
an instrument of dialogue rather than a one-way means of communication as journals have traditionally been. The contents of the journal
would follow the needs and interests of its readers. However, Berkenkotter and Huckin's analysis of the journal over the period 1977–1988
shows that it gradually evolved into a traditional-style journal, eventually becoming cited in *The Arts and Humanities Citation Index*. In
order to achieve legitimacy, to attract the biggest names in the field
to publish in the journal it had to shift in the direction of other journals, becoming more formal, with longer articles which looked much
the same as those found elsewhere and so on. With a name change to
Reader: Essays in Reader-Oriented Theory, Criticism and Pedagogy,

the journal became virtually indistinguishable from any other academic publication. The editors had acquiesced to the dominant conventions of appropriateness.

▶ Commentary

In both these cases structural forces – ones which lend consistency and relative permanence to social practices – can be seen in play, for example, in the dominant traditions of research publications. Agency was manifest initially, in that these dominant traditions were challenged, but eventually structure predominated. Power can be seen in play too, of course, manifested in the actions of editors, as can the discursive genres which hold sway. These are expressed in the 'market' structures in the scientific community which condition the success or otherwise of the *Reader* and in the discursive forms which are considered acceptable.

A striking example from my South African research of the unconsidered adoption of standards of appropriateness and inappropriateness in terms of practices, decisions, and choices in a particular context related to the use of graduate teaching assistants (GTAs). Some respondents said that GTAs were only ever used in year one of the degree ('of course!'). Tutorials were highly structured and GTAs were given a clear script and set of tasks for students to do. One respondent explained this:

> At first year on this campus we believe very strongly in the tutorial which they don't on the other campuses. It was the one thing we were not prepared to compromise on – If the tutorial in the first year was done away with by the common curriculum it would really compromise us . . . . A tutorial is a first year session run by a postgraduate and they discuss work students prepare the week beforehand. It's the only time they are getting, not quite one to one but fairly individual attention. We can spot weaknesses and so on. They don't have an equivalent on the other campuses: they did away with tutorials as having only a nuisance value, being a luxury. They don't use postgraduates in that way, supporting the teaching of first-years.

Others, however, said that GTAs were only used in the second and third years ('of course!'). Academic staff delivered the lectures, and GTAs led fairly unstructured discussions about them in seminars with students. Here were completely contrasting sets of conventions about what was appropriate and inappropriate use of GTAs, conventions themselves founded on a set of tacit assumptions.

▶ Vignette: Assessment as social practice (adapted from Shay, 2003, 2004)

The assessment of student work is usually seen as a professional practice ideally founded upon criteria which offer a degree of robustness, objectivity, reliability, and universality to professional judgements. Complex sets of apparatus are often put in place to ensure that this is the case, including assessment criteria, double marking, moderation events, and the rest. Quality assurance organisations at the national level are usually very keen to see such apparatus working effectively.

An alternative view is to consider assessment as social practice: that is, founded on taken-for-granted recurrent ways of acting together in the world which articulate and reinforce sets of values and attitudes in a provisionally stable way. Seen from this perspective assessment is situationally contingent, rooted in local cultures and reliable and robust only in terms of sets of assumptions, attitudes, and values which are, in part at least, localised.

Shay (2003) came to the conclusion that this latter view was the more accurate one in her study of the assessment practices of two disciplinary communities, those in the Engineering and Humanities faculties in a single South African university. Academics in these two faculties developed what Bourdieu calls a 'feel for the game' of assessment, a tacit understanding of appropriateness which was socially constructed and acquired; and so more than just a matter of personal opinion, or prejudice. This took some time for novices to acquire, and the acquisition process was achieved through a process of socialisation, not explicit transmission. As one Engineering interviewee noted, 'No one has to tell you anything, you learn. You are in a place.' What is going on, according to Shay, is the acquisition of a set of interpretive matrices, of frameworks which make the assessment task relatively straightforward to insiders.

There are two key points about this:

1. The 'feel for the game' is quite different in different communities of practice. Though Shay doesn't explicitly compare the Engineering and the Humanities faculties it is clear that they would have developed different sets of interpretive matrices. Disciplinary and sub-disciplinary differences as well as the 'social construction of reality' locally lead to such differences.

2. But the immediate context of academics together determining a grade for an assignment was a site at which there was negotiation, even conflict, about the social practice of assessment. This served to moderate what would otherwise be a structuralist account of individual academics simply acquiring then putting into practice a set of tacit understandings and conventions about assessment. Thus, for example, a student's supervisor may enter into negotiation with other assessors about the relative weight to be given to the process the student engaged in while writing their assignment as compared to the product in front of the assessors. Such arguments arise largely because of the differing functions that assessment performs, many of which are in tension with each other. Issues of personal and professional identity are particularly important during these times of contest.

So, underpinning assessment practices are sets of values and attitudes which, in their articulation in recurrent assessment practices, both reinforce and are reinforced by the cultural milieu in which they exist. Indeed, assessment practices can act as a powerful signal for the standpoints valued by an academic community, marking differences between them and other disciplinary communities on their borders.

Shay writes,

> What I discovered as I interviewed nearly thirty academic assessors from different ends of the disciplinary spectrum was that the appeal to intuition as the basis for academic judgement was not uncommon ... 'I'm not going to tie myself to these criteria. I can't' ... 'I don't have a mind that splits into seven bits'
>
> (Shay, 2003, p. 95)

Another feature of assessors' interpretive matrices that emerged was experience, that is, the extent to which individual markers have been socialized into the community's 'ways of seeing'. As one experienced member of staff noted, 'It's relatively easy to decide whether a project deserves a first, second or third class pass'. He conceded however, 'But not the first time'. . . . One member of staff gave a personal illustration of how his socialization as a marker happened. As a new member of staff he recalls feeling very unsure of his marking initially. In his first year he was "higher" than everyone, his second year he was "lower". A senior member of staff assured him that this "pattern" happens to everyone. 'This is the way in which people learn to adjust their marking,' they told him. 'You get in, you see 'oh this is how it's done', and you change ...' . . . . Thus one of the explanations for why (in some cases) such wide discrepancies emerged between markers was that new staff had not yet developed a common 'professional vision' of the community. . . . The problem is further exacerbated for new staff by the lack of any explicit rules or guidelines. As one member of staff assessing for the first time recalled, 'The impression that we were given as new supervisors, is that, it's left to academic feeling, that you decide how you want to mark'

(Shay, 2004, p. 9)

▶ **Commentary**

Shay's concept of interpretive matrices is very closely connected to the notions of 'tacit assumptions' that are set out here . These matrices guide the practices that are employed, in this case in relation to the assessment of student work. Conventions of appropriateness in relation to that work become established. Work which lacks congruence with the interpretive matrices developed is considered to be inappropriate, of low quality, and so likely to receive a lower mark. Tacit assumptions, conventions of appropriateness, and recurrent practices are, like the other moments, intimately intertwined.

Power relations

We have seen already that relations of power permeate interactions, and that some discourses, sets of assumptions, and other moments hold sway while others have less-powerful social locations. In the vignette on pp. 93–94 we saw the power of structures gradually take effect on the practices and discourses involving academic journals. The more immediate operation of power (and the attempt to subvert it) also happened in that instance: power in the hands of gatekeepers, the editors, and reviewers of June Davis' paper. Davis takes a very unusual step in her first letter to the editor of the *Journal of Infection and Immunity*: she suggests names of potential referees. Berkenkotter and Huckin explain this:

In an interview, Davis revealed that she had made this move to circumvent getting for a reviewer a colleague who was in competition with her and who was in a larger and more prestigious lab. This colleague had previously written negative reviews of her grant proposals and papers. Because the price of receiving a positive review from this colleague had been to 'cut him in' on important projects in her research, she hoped that, by this rather aggressive strategy, she could avoid getting him as a referee.

(1995, p. 68)

Individuals, groups, and social structures exercise power, and be said to 'have' power on an ongoing basis. Of course, the operation of power by individuals and groups relates in important ways to issues of gender, ethnicity, disability, and other socially structured relations of inequality and privilege. Because of this it is itself structured and patterned in significant ways as well as being more dynamic and momentary, as post-structural theory tends to argue.

But what *is* power?

Lukes (1974, 2005) distinguishes three dimensions of power and the way it is exercised:

1. Individuals or groups securing outcomes or behaviours that operate in their interests, as they perceive them.

    > this first, one-dimensional, view of power involves a focus on behaviour in the making of decisions on issues over which there is an observable conflict of (subjective) interests
    >
    > (Lukes, 2005, p. 19)

    The example above, involving June Davis, illustrates this dimension.
2. The setting of agendas and exclusion of issues from the agenda. This dimension of power also involves things that are made *not* to happen as well as those which are made to happen because they are placed on the agenda. Some things are made to be seen as 'just normal' and others as inconceivable, undesirable, and nonsensical. Thus one set of values, attitudes, and practices is privileged above others.

    > the two-dimensional view of power ... allows for consideration of the ways in which decisions are prevented from being taken on potential issues over which there is an observable conflict of (subjective) interests
    >
    > (Lukes, 2005, p. 25)

    In the vignette on pp. 93–94, the gradual shift in discourse, practice, and conventions of appropriateness of the journal which set out to challenge these is an example here.
3. Discursive capture: discourse is used to shape not only what is and is not on the agenda but what can and cannot be thought about and expressed and what can be done. This form of power operates in the

real, not just subjective, interests of individuals and groups according to Lukes. Here an act of imagination is required to see how things could be done differently.

> the three-dimensional view of power involves a thoroughgoing critique of the behavioural focus of the first two views as too individualistic and allows for consideration the many ways in which potential issues are kept out of politics, whether through the operation of social forces and institutional practices or through individuals' decisions. This, moreover, can occur in the absence of observable conflict, which may have been successfully averted
>
> (Lukes, 2005, p. 29)

This last view of power in operation is close to what Bourdieu (1998) refers to as 'symbolic violence'. For Bourdieu, symbolic violence is the capacity to impose the means for comprehending and adapting to the social world by representing economic and political power in disguised, taken-for-granted forms. This is a subtle, euphemised, invisible mode of domination that prevents domination from being recognised as such and is therefore considered naturally legitimate. Effectively, the dominated are complicit in their own domination. It is a 'de-faced' theory of power, not operated by individual people (with faces) but is systemic in nature, deriving from symbolic systems.

Foucault, by contrast (1980), uses the notion of the micro-physics of power, by which he means localised mechanisms, techniques, and practices enacted within the workplace (Ball, 1990) and calls for careful study of its operation there. It is not difficult to find examples of all three dimensions of power operating at the level of 'micro-physics'. Of course, all social groups engage in the transmission and application of power of various sorts: from simple brute force, making people do things which they do not want to do to more subtle agenda-setting or circumstance-changing practices. Daily life is permeated with symbols and symbolic systems which shape practices and the way the world is apprehended. In universities the shape that power takes, the way it flows, and how it surfaces will vary from place to place and time to time. There are trends, however, linked to wider social forces. Reay, for example, takes a very dim view of the effect of social forces on higher education and contrasts higher education today with a happier age:

> Processes of corporatisation, casualisation, commodification, contractualism and compliance work against, and undermine, collegiality and cooperation. What has happened to "the community of scholars" in the new corporatist era? I suggest that it has been reconfigured as an

upper echelon of elite, predominantly male, academics serviced by an army of casualised teaching, research and administrative staff, a poor shadow of what the community should be.

(Reay, 2004, p. 34)

Of course, it is very common to find today's situation unfavourably compared with some previous 'golden age', the characteristics of which are more aspirational than actual. The operation of power will always be found, with different forms and with different effects. And of course the wider, structural operation of power flows through and into universities and teaching and learning regimes.

▶ **Vignette: Power and the common curriculum in a South African University**

The application of power was very evident in the newly merged institution I studied. One of three departments in the same discipline, law, quickly mobilised available resources to make sure that their approach to the curriculum and its delivery was the one to be adopted and that that discipline became centred on *their* campus.

We were desperate to stay here – if we could swing it we would try to. I think we had an advantage in that they [law on campus X] had very few resources, very limited library facilities in particular, and we had all the access to databases and online stuff

When I think back to how we came to persuade them, it was about people: persuasive personalities taking the initiative. In truth we had sway of numbers. So when we said 'look we've got a great course at first year level' (and we did our homework in advance) it was very hard for campus X to argue against it . . . There were a number of strong personalities in our department who really pushed their particular teaching interest and research interest

You had your people who clearly saw it as their territory trying to persuade everybody else. It was power plays, horse trading, "we will give you this if you give us that". Usually one dominant player took the lead. There are individual personalities, powerful personalities, strong players, who feel they own their specialisms and tend to dominate. They are going to squeeze out specialists who are less able to make their case. Coming from a position of authority they came in and laid it down – 'we've always done it like this' – and they intimidated people.

▶ Commentary

In this example we can see all three dimensions of Lukes' analysis of power in play. Dimension 1 is evident as individuals dominate, intimidate, and argue to manipulate the outcomes of the discussion in a way which is in their interests. Dimension 2 is also apparent as the 'strong personalities' push the agenda of the discussion into areas of brand identity and market demand. Dimension 3 is related to that: the discussion was dominated (in this account at least) by a discourse of the market and quality provision, mobilised in the interests of one of the groups in these discussions.

Subjectivities in interaction

Individual 'identity' can sometimes be seen as separate from the social context in which it is located. However, sociocultural theory adopts a situated approach to identity, seeing an intimate connection between social locale and the individual. Maclean adopts this position, suggesting that people

> are positioned by the actions they undertake as group members, by their relative centrality to the group's activities, by the power they wield and the restrictions placed on them as a result of group membership, and by the boundaries which separate members of a group from members of another... Membership of a group helps to constitute identity, but it is an identity which is restated and renegotiated with each action.
>
> (Maclean, 1996, p. 172)

Maclean's use of the word 'positioned' is illuminating. This puts the focus on the interactions that go on in the development of subjectivities, capturing the power dimension in this too. Furthermore, 'positioning' can be accomplished by the individual themselves and by others – it can be reflexive or structured. The use of the transitive verb 'position' avoids the concretising and fixed overtones of the word 'identity', and the suggestions of multiple fragmented selves in its plural, 'identities'. Hall recognises this:

> [Identity is]...not an essence but a positioning. Hence there is always a politics of identity, a politics of position... Identity should be seen as a 'production' which is never complete, always in process, and always constituted within, not outside, representation.
>
> (Hall, 1990, pp. 22 and 226).

The notion of subjectivity as positioned can accommodate the affective dimension of the self as well as self-concept and other aspects usually associated with the term 'identity'. Subjectivity conceived in this way is the result of a highly interactive process, one which McDermott and Varenne describe graphically as people 'hammering each other into shape' (1995, p. 326). In this view culture both constitutes and is constituted by the many voices of people bringing each other into life and being made significant by others. These voices are polyphonous, sometimes harmonious, often not. Very often they are contradictory. Culture is not only about consensus, but also about 'hammering a world', a rather more vigorous, contentious, and painful experience than Geertz's metaphor of 'spinning webs of significance'.

Just as organisations are not 'birth-marked' with a particular culture (p. 13), neither are individuals 'birth-marked' by an identity according to this position. To see an individual just in terms of their gender, their extraversion, their self-concept in relation to higher education or some other permanent, non-situated dimension fails to capture the dynamic, relational, and sometimes-conflictual character of subjectivity. To understand the constitution of subjectivity we need to see how the self is implicated in moment-by-moment interactions, and to see the significance of discourse and of power in this (Parker, 2000). Giddens suggests that what he calls 'self-identity' becomes a reflexively organised endeavour which consists of sustaining coherent, yet continuously revised, biographical narratives (1991, p. 5).

This understanding of positioning is reflected in the data I collected in fine-grained studies of academics and their contexts. The following respondent is an example. She was interviewed for a study of academics newly arrived at their university to study the process of organisational socialisation (Trowler and Knight, 2000). She demonstrates both the agentic character of subjectivity and the importance of structures such as ideologies which contain that agency:

Because you are in a competitive university world you have to actually construct yourself to be good at all three of these things [research, teaching and administration] . . . You have to present yourself as . . . being good in all these three areas and then it's actually hard to take yourself back out of that and say 'well what originally was I interested in', or 'what did I think I was good at?' . . . You have to have this very fluid identity.

(Respondent 2, new academics study, female, Women's Studies, English chartered university)

This quote illustrates well Ivanic's point that subjectivity is a site of tension not only between individuals but between individual agency and structural forces:

> A critical view of the social construction of identity not only recognizes the powerful influence of dominant ideologies in controlling and constraining people's view of themselves, but also recognizes the possibility of struggle for alternative definitions.
>
> (Ivanic, 1998, p. 13)

The next respondent, from a different study (this one an ethnographic study of change in an English university, referred to as 'NewU'), illustrates this potential for struggle:

> One of the first things that hit me was my lack of autonomy as a lecturer in the system and I ... got a bit of a nickname when I first came here because my colleagues in sociology kept talking about disempowerment. Every time I came in they would say 'oh here she comes to talk about disempowerment' because that was my major feeling and that was what I kept saying to them. I feel really disempowered within this context.
>
> (Respondent 31, NewU, in the study published as Trowler, 1998, female, sociology)

Another respondent, again from the study of organisational socialisation described above, said,

> [I asked myself] how much work does the University actually do in terms of partnership with other people? ... I didn't come to this university as a blank slate [but] ... when I say something ... what I have to say isn't considered. ... I went to the Dean and 'I said I don't want to be socialized into this system. I don't know how long I'm going to last here because there are so many things that are against who I am, in conflict with who I am as an individual' ... [There are areas in which I] can't say the kind of things I really want to. If I really start on the meat and potatoes, the real essence, the core where some of this stuff is coming from, then it's like all of a sudden the person is gone.
>
> (Respondent 17, new academics study, female minority ethnic group member, teacher education, Canadian university)

From a sociocultural perspective, then, cultures and subjectivities are intimately linked. Socialisation involves not just a passive process of enculturation of the individual but an accommodative process which involves elements of change at both the individual and the cultural level.

Thinking about the individual within his or her organisational context, one can use the metaphor of the organisation being the anvil against which our subjectivities are re-shaped. As Goffman puts it (1961, p. 320),

> Our sense of being a person can come from being drawn into a wider social unit; our sense of selfhood can arise through the little ways in which we resist the pull. Our status is backed by the solid buildings of the world; while our sense of personal identity often resides in the cracks.

Teaching and learning regimes are socially created but they comprise a number of individuals whose individuality is not lost within them. As people interact within the workgroup the interpersonal 'hammering' referred to above goes on: personal and professional identities (or subjectivities) are negotiated, sustained, attacked, and defended.

> It is now a commonplace that a person's social identity is not unitary but a configuration of identities; to that we can see the external negotiation of difference with others as continuous with – and rooted in – the internal negotiation of difference in the struggle to constitute the self.
>
> (Fairclough, 1996, p. 8)

Identity construction is therefore something of an accomplishment, something achieved processually. However, this production process can also involve consensus as well as conflict. For Bernstein this is the case, with subjectivities being rooted in

> the dynamic interface between individual careers and the social or collective base...Identity arises out of a particular social order, through relations which the identity enters into with other identities of reciprocal recognition, support, mutual legitimization and finally through collective purpose.
>
> (Bernstein, 1996, p. 73)

This depiction may put too functionalist a gloss on the situation. As I suggested earlier, neither consensus nor conflict tells the whole story about social interactions. Neither consensus nor conflict is merely ethnographic 'dazzle' (Fox, 1980) the one subsidiary to the other. Identity as an accomplishment is born of *both* 'mutual legitimization' and 'interpersonal hammering'. From an individual perspective this history of subjectivity development results in a life story about the self.

The defence of subjectivity built up over time can be very significant for teaching, learning, and assessment practices, where dimensions of the personal impinge on practice: the professor who defends academic integrity to her dying breath even at the cost of confusing students; the 'student fundamentalist' whose identity is bound up with the perceived interests of students; the researcher who sees the discussion of teaching as intellectually demeaning; and so on.

In the South African context 'personalities' are very significant in change processes: the new black vice chancellor and his very particular approach to management; key political figures, their personal predilections and sets of issues; the individuals who are capable but did not get the job because they are male, white, and middle-class. Subjectivities are very significant elements in the backstories there too, and are very much shaped by the history and context of South Africa, especially the history of struggle against the apartheid regime and one's role (or narratives about one's role) in that. Context and subjectivity interact, each shaping the other, and the character of the multiple subjectivities that dynamically coexist in a teaching and learning regime has important implications for practices, issues, and agendas as well as for the shape of and divisions within a TLR.

The study of the newly merged institution in South Africa showed whether particular individuals can be powerful or not in different contexts and this is partly to do with interaction of subjectivities. Here a respondent comments on one individual who fought strongly for a rigidly enforced common curriculum across the campuses of a new institution:

In any merger situation you have the philosophical issues and you have the personalities. We had a lulu of a personality! I don't think I'm exaggerating when I say he was a little Hitler. He was in charge of disciplines X and Y . . . . But he was so obstructionist and political that the academics in discipline Y couldn't get on with him – several of them left.

We found out in our first few meetings with him that he was the arch-commonality man – We must have common tests, common curriculum, common everything. And anyone who didn't believe in this philosophy, didn't agree with him, had to be reported. He was so authoritarian with his staff that it meant that they couldn't discuss the common curriculum freely with us. I said 'do you know what this [attempt to standardise] means logistically, and do you know what it means to people's autonomy to teach what they want?' So when we came to working out the common curriculum in discipline X it wasn't academically-based, with a careful analysis of our country's needs, the trends, students' needs and the nature of the discipline. It was personality-based, the cut and thrust of personality.

▶ Vignette: When things go wrong (adapted from Warner and Palfreyman, 2003)

During the 1980s a remarkably similar set of events occurred in a number of colleges and universities in the United Kingdom involving significant crises. Typically, the stories involved much human drama, stress, forced resignations, and restructuring, usually ending in a financial crisis after which a new leadership leads the institution to restructuring or to merger. The dramatis personae and plots of these stories have remarkable similarities: a forceful institutional leader with very firm ideas who has difficulty differentiating between himself (almost always 'him') and the institution; a largely supine Board of Governors with one or two strong figures who are cronies of the leader; a cowed and fearful staff; foreign adventures involving delivery of courses abroad untroubled by quality control procedures or the usual checks and balances of institutional governance.

Thus at University College, Cardiff (from 1987), Southampton Institute (from 1988), Swansea Institute of Higher Education (from 1989), Coventry Technical College (from 1989), and elsewhere the story played itself out. And of course good stories always need a strong villain. Cardiff's leader into crisis, Dr Cecil Bevan, had slogans including 'Rules are for fools', 'we want to expand like hell', and (in the face of dire warnings from the funding council) had a determination to 'keep buggering on'(KBO) (Warner and Palfreyman, 2003, chapter 2). At Southampton very rapid but unregulated expansion in various foreign locations and a looming financial crisis led to considerable unease among staff and others. An independent auditor found that 'in response to the question "why do you not speak up and express your views forcefully on academic matters or on institutional matters?" the response given by a large number of staff from the most senior to the most junior was fear' (reported in Warner and Palfreyman, 2003,p. 65). At Swansea a subsequent leader of the institution says of his predecessor who led it into crisis: 'It could be argued that Dr Stockdale was a man of some vision and foresight...Unfortunately almost no one, including the generality of staff and members of the board of governors...knew about Dr Stockdale's activities' (ibid., p. 91). They included large amounts of international travel – including to Kenya 18 times – in connection with an unapproved strategy of course delivery abroad.

▶ Commentary

Eventually, the obvious question gets asked: 'what went wrong?' The answer is usually 'pilot error'; the leader was obviously to blame: he lost the plot. And yet such an answer fails to address the question 'why there were so many instances of crisis at around the same time with so many similarities?' The '[not so] great man' theory of disaster does not hold up in this regard. The political and financial context of higher education at the time, the pressures on institutions to 'chase the dollar', the liberalisation of controls on institutions, and a range of other structural and contextual factors mean that the subjectivities in place tended to be of a particular kind. Although the actions of individuals are the most palpable causes of failure, they themselves are conditioned and constrained by wider but less obvious structural characteristics.

▶ Vignette: The B.Ed. Honours team, South Africa (adapted from Mathieson, 2004)

Nine of the ten members of a B.Ed. programme team in a South African university were interviewed about their attitudes towards the programme and to teaching and learning generally. All had come to this university's School of Education late in their careers and had a wide range of experience in non-academic environments prior to their current posts. Most had worked as teachers and had considerable classroom experience. Four of them had experience in non-governmental organisations. Their disciplinary backgrounds were varied, including educational psychology, English and drama, applied language studies, and science. Only three of the nine interviewees identified their disciplinary background in education as the primary influence on their approach to teaching and learning. Asked about the primary influences on their approaches to teaching and learning, two of the group of nine identified Freire, two Bernstein, and two Vygotsky. All had trained as teachers.

Taking on an academic identity had come slowly for most. Many of the group saw themselves first as educators and only secondly as academics (including research and other roles). Two of the nine resisted the adoption of an academic identity and considered themselves more oriented to practice than to theory. Four of the nine people interviewed had some sense of being an outsider to the BA programme, while eight expressed some sense of being an outsider to the programme, to the university, or to the School of Education. There was thus a considerable empathy with students who feel marginalised and awkward in the academic world.

For five of the interviewees the sense of being South African was a strong influence on their approach to teaching and learning. The sense of a South African identity was experienced in complex and personal ways. Six of the nine were white women and for this group their sense of a South African identity appeared to have been approached tangentially. Some had experienced oppression and marginalisation because of gender or sexual orientation and had come to link this over time to other forms of social oppression, leading to empathy with the marginalised and disadvantaged and their struggles for an identity.

Despite the differences between them, there were many common characteristics within this group. A number of interviewees pointed to the coherence in approach between the B.Ed. Honours programme and the School of Education more broadly. There was also felt to be a strong shared perspective among academic staff in the School of Education, and a collegial atmosphere where one interviewee identified a strong sense of being 'at home'. This perspective was based on the School's agenda for educational transformation, which was rooted in a strong commitment to provide access to continuing education to rural teachers who would not normally have access to university. The School of Education was critically engaged with government policy in this respect.

Seven of the nine emphasised the importance of a student-centred approach towards their work. Two of the nine, however, were concerned that progressivist pedagogies further disadvantaged the already disadvantaged black students because they under-emphasised the importance of imparting knowledge to students. From this perspective literacy and knowledge were linked with power. A progressivist, learner-centred pedagogy that failed to teach students the discourses of knowledge served only to reinforce social inequalities by leaving the students in a trap of their own limited access to expert knowledge. It was, in their words, a 'pedagogy of benign neglect and benevolent inertia'. For these two the explicit teaching of grammar and writing was important – students had to be moved from everyday discourses to specialist discourses. Another interviewee stressed the important role of the expert in providing content and in prompting, in asking the right questions. This interviewee argued that academics have to make evaluative judgements; they cannot abdicate responsibility for pointing to the correct answer.

All of the team who were interviewed were committed to the project of 'transformation' in South Africa: redressing the disadvantages for black populations which were the legacy of apartheid. Yet the academics teaching on the programme seemed torn between expressions of concern and empathy with student difficulties, rooted in the structured disadvantages of South African society, and at the same time a sense of frustration with the poor quality of some student work. Two interviewees noted that they had changed their approaches to teaching and learning in response to the students on the programme. One saw this as a positive experience, involving being forced to think more deeply about the challenges of student writing and reading. Another saw it more negatively. The lack of feedback from students had pushed her into spoon-feeding students with information, an approach which contradicted her philosophies of teaching and learning.

▶ **Commentary**

This vignette again illustrates the relationship between subjectivities and agency on the one hand and the contextual characteristics which condition those subjectivities and limit that agency on the other. Some of these academics were struggling, in the post-apartheid context of South Africa, to reconcile sometimes contradictory sets of beliefs. Some of these issues cut to the core of their concepts of themselves and of their professional roles. In other contexts, where the pressures for transformation and the legacies of the past were not so evident, it would be more likely that 'comfortable' subjectivities and associated beliefs and values could continue to exist without challenge.

Codes of signification

Codes of signification refer to socially constructed layers of meaning and emotional response to texts, signs, and practices. They are evoked by particular 'signs' in specific contexts – words, phrases, pictures, activities. Activities, organisations, terms, concepts, and things not only have meanings attributed to them in a cognitive sense but are layered with affective (emotional) significance. Thus the term 'quality', and organisations and people associated with it in a particular university, may evoke responses of delight, fear, worry, stress, or something else. Dirkx (2001) rightly says that there has tended to be a 'rationalist doctrine' associated both with educational practice and with the study of it, yet emotional responses permeate education as they do everything else. A growing body of literature has begun to look at the emotional dimension in education (for a summary see Moore and Kuol, 2007), but this has tended to focus on the dynamics of emotion in the classroom rather than on academic staff. But emotion is important in meaning-making in work groups and their reception of change:

> The process of meaning making ... is essentially imaginative and extrarational, rather than merely reflective and rational. Emotionally charged images ... provide the opportunity for a more profound access to the world by inviting a deeper understanding of ourselves in relationship with it.
>
> (Dirkx, 2001, p. 64)

Such responses are not simply individual in nature – they are socially conditioned as workgroups meet new circumstances, discuss them, and respond to them. The development of emotional intelligence (Goleman, 1995, 1998) is usually seen to be an individual task, resulting in purely individual competence, or lack of it. The concepts of emotional literacy, emotional competence, and emotional intelligence are all rooted in the individual. Such an approach ignores other emotional geographies. Hargreaves (1998) takes issue with this psychologism, noting that situating emotions only in the individual ignores broader structural factors. Thus, for example, changes to the nature of regulation of teaching and social changes can lead to greater emotional commitments among teachers, and increasing levels of 'burnout', as more and more demands are made on them under intensified and extended working conditions.

Hargreaves is right that macro changes are important, but so are conditions at the meso level. Denzin (1984) focuses here, arguing that 'emotional understanding' comes about when we share feelings in common with others and when shared feelings and emotional experiences recur in long-standing relationships. However, this kind of emotional intersubjectivity is only sometimes found at the workgroup level, and only over some issues. Denzin, like many of the writers on organisational cultures, has a tendency to consensualise. Emotions are as much about conflict and struggle as they are about shared feelings. Again, both consensus and conflict operate and both are equally 'real'.

Crossman (2007) notes that for many writers on emotions trying to classify them and relate consistent effects to them in any way is a futile exercise. Rather, as Wittgenstein (1982) suggests, constructivist and more ideographic approaches provide a more fruitful way of understanding them. This approach assumes that individuals 'appraise and respond to social contexts as a part of meaning-making and interpersonal process, and assumes that emotions are learned and cultural mediated' (Crossman, 2007, p. 314).

In this way the layers of emotion and meaning encapsulated in the phrase 'codes of signification' are mediated by specific cultural contexts as well as sometimes resulting from resonances from an individual's past as well as from associations with their individual beliefs and values (Crossman, 2007, p. 320).

As workgroups engage on common projects over time these codes are socially constructed, negotiated, and sometimes contested in such a way as to make them unique to that workgroup, at least in some respects. They are not fixed in a 'sign' but in the sign-in-context. Take for example, the sign 'research':

> research signifies as a high-level activity but only when it is embodied in lecturing staff. When it is embodied in the female contract researcher it becomes reconstituted as a low-level activity.
>
> (Reay, 2000, p. 15)

Such responses are often emotional, involving powerful stereotypes and are closely related to tacit assumptions. Advertisers encourage audiences to develop and mobilise carefully built codes of signification in relation to products through the process of branding and in other ways. In teaching and learning regimes, by contrast, codes of signification develop more serendipitously. Concepts and practices like 'lectures', 'multiple-choice examinations', 'problem-based learning', and others become heavily loaded and so evoke a response in terms of emotion and connotations. Any innovation will elicit responses of this sort – and that in itself will condition subsequent actions.

In the South African merged institution study it was clear that different campuses mobilised codes of signification about each other which were wrapped up with evaluations of quality, race issues, assumptions about their students and practices, and so on. In a sense the extent to which these codes match the 'reality' is not particularly significant; such subjective responses have real effects even though they may be based on stereotypical views, even upon racist assumptions in some cases. This is illustrated by the following quote:

> As we merged . . . . the first thing that became apparent was that UniY didn't have the same academic standards and the same regard for teaching as we did . . . . The idea was that we would form one big school of [our discipline] across all the campuses. The heads of [that discipline] met together to discuss the merger – but it quickly became apparent that no-one understood what the others were doing. So even between UniX and College Z there was a cultural difference . . . And then we had the UniY scenario where they were MILES behind us. And the biggest problem we had was – how do you tell somebody that they are not very good? . . . When you have different institutions with different academic

cultures it's very hard for people to believe that they are not doing the best job.... We have a strong culture of teaching and learning but University Y to tell you the truth had no culture at all. However, they have now adopted most of our courses, but that was hard work. So now we've got a common curriculum in [our discipline] which is very very learner based.... One of the best things we've done is the optional Saturday morning tutorials. We go along with some PhD and MA students and give extra help to the kids working through the workbooks. The staff in UniY said 'if we did that our students wouldn't come because our students are different from your students'. And that's been the big thing with the merger – everybody thinks they and their students are different.

▶ Vignette: Courtesans and codes of signification in afternoon carriage rides (adapted from Hickman, 2003)

The caléche was the lightest and quickest of all the carriages then in fashion, and was designed for one person only, an open landau for summer use. The Empress's favourite, a daumont, on the other hand...had room inside for two.... To be alone in a caléche, the swiftest and most skiff-like of carriages, was not considered indelicate, but to the sensibility of the time, there was something decidedly indecorous in sitting, alone, in a carriage where there is room for two. The slower pace of these bigger and more cumbersome vehicles only emphasised the impropriety. Perhaps oddly, given these extremely delicate sensibilities, it was considered perfectly respectable for a woman to drive herself: the crucial point was that she should drive fast enough. To those who were acutely tuned to the subtleties of these parades, there were other clues and caveats too. Even the way a woman sat in her carriage, and how she arranged the folds of her dress, might speak volumes about her.... By these most delicate of nuances it was perfectly possible for actresses and demi-mondaines to advertise their charms only too clearly on their afternoon carriage rides" (237–238).

▶ Commentary

This small vignette, well outside the field of higher education, is included to illustrate the use of subtle signs which convey, to the culturally literate, significant messages. Cultural context and cultural literacy is all-important here. To the modern eye the subtlety is discussed by Hickman in women's behaviour, dress, and mode of transport during these afternoon carriage rides in public parks would be completely opaque. Similarly, subtle signs with strong significance exist in every culture but tend to be simply taken for granted to those immersed within their cultural context.

▶ Conclusion

This chapter has set out the eight moments of teaching and learning regimes. The claimed usefulness of this scheme lies in its ability to assist the analysis of different contexts, and any proposed change initiative, taking each of the moments in turn. It is important, however, to re-state the fact that this separation into parts is only done for analytical purposes. There are interconnections and overlapping characteristics across all of these moments. It is possible to envisage a situation in which almost all of the moments of a teaching and learning regime are aligned. Such a situation would occur in an institution in which managerialism was the dominant ethos and where the discursive repertoires in use reflected that ideological stance. Power of different sorts would lie firmly in the hands of the top team, though distributed in a highly conditional way to the periphery. Recurrent practices in terms of interactions with students would reflect a managerialist ethos: they would be treated as 'customers', and the educational ideology in play would largely be a vocationalist one. The main objective would centre around employability and the curriculum would be 'delivered' in standard ways. There would be little or no opposition to the managerialist hegemony in this institution because the way they 'do things around there' would be considered 'just normal'. The discursive repertoires, implicit theories of teaching and learning, subjectivities, and the rest found in local workgroups would largely reflect the managerialism of the wider institution.

In such situations one could say that there was a strong culture. As noted above, according to some management theorists this is a highly desirable state; strong cultures (meaning evident, coherent, and hegemonic) are a characteristic of successful organisations (Deal and Kennedy, 1982; Peters and Waterman, 1982). The assumption in such work is that the strength of the culture leads to business success, not the other way around (though one could just as well argue that the causality runs in that direction). The empirical basis of such claims has been questioned, in particular the examples of successful organisations quoted have often subsequently run into trouble. Perhaps they were not so successful after all, or were successful at a particular time and in certain circumstances.

However, to have so aligned a situation in a university is both highly unlikely and almost certainly undesirable. Willmott (1993) makes the point that a monocultural university is virtually a contradiction in terms: universities by their nature are dialogical; they thrive on dialogue, intellectual contest, and debate. Without it the life of the mind will die there.

5 Organisational Shape and Processes: Learning Architectures, Enhancement Cultures

> Organizations can be understood as shaping local versions of broader societal and locally developed cultural manifestations in a multitude of ways. Organizational cultures are...best understood not as unitary wholes or as stable sets of subcultures but as mixtures of cultural manifestations of different levels and kinds. Even in seemingly homogeneous and stable organizations such as universities cultural configurations are multiple, complex and shifting.
>
> *(Alvesson, 2002, pp. 190–191)*

> ...evidence all points to the same conclusion. Unless central reforms address the context of teaching and learning, as well as capacity building...within the context of external support, then aspirations of reform will never be realised.
>
> *(Hopkins, 2002, p. 9)*

Almost every study of higher education, whatever the focus, has shown that institutional context has a significant bearing on practices. This is true of studies of the implementation of national policies (for example, Morgan-Klein and Murphy, 2002) as well as impact studies, for example, of teaching courses for academic staff (Prosser *et al.*, 2006). So, though I have stressed that teaching and learning regimes are open to cultural currents of all sorts, including from wider society, gender and ethnic socialisation, and so on, it is clear that institutional context has a particularly significant role to play when considering the enhancement of teaching and learning.

It is of course very difficult to generalise about institutions of higher education or even about universities. Nowadays higher education goes on in many contexts, in further education, in private companies, and in institutions containing the word 'university' but with hugely different characteristics. In writing this chapter I aim to pitch the discussion at a level which would apply to these different contexts, though I may not always have been successful in this.

The chapter first unpicks the different ways in which we can understand universities as organisations, proposing one way of modelling them in particular. On the basis of this it moves on to suggest ways in which universities can enhance organisational learning through developing appropriate 'learning architectures'. Finally, it suggests that such architectures need to be suffused with enhancement cultures if initiatives to change for the better are to catch hold and succeed.

▶ Ways of understanding organisational cultures

In attempting to conceptualise the nature of a university it is possible of course to use the same *moments* used in previous chapters as analytical devices at this level of analysis too. So, each university would be considered in terms of the particular configuration of recurrent practices, power relations, implicit theories, and so on. Towards the end of the chapter I will make some comments about the relevance of that way of seeing to thinking about universities as whole institutions. But, while attractive, the complexities in doing this at the institutional level are such that much analytical power would be lost. This is because the cultural complexity of universities is considerable. They are best characterised in terms of possessing a multiple cultural configuration, with many departmental and sub-departmental units generating distinctive ways of being and ways of seeing. I elaborate on this below, but first examine some alternative ways in which the cultures of higher education institutions have been conceptualised.

As we saw in Chapter 1, organisational cultures are usually conceptualised in the literature in one of four broad ways:

1. As belonging to one of a limited number of possible types. This so-called 'nomothetic' approach is a dominant one. A four-box matrix of organisational types is usually offered. Associated with this approach is what is sometimes called 'corporate culturism' (Willmott, 1993). Authors such as Deal and Kennedy (1982) and Beckhard and Pritchard (1992) argue that changing the culture from one type to another, 'changing the essence' as Beckhard and Pritchard style it, is a good way to enhance effectiveness, and that this can be achieved by using the right managerial techniques. This approach is rooted in simplistic notions of motivation and change at the personal level: behaviouristic and social learning models which see individuals as easily influenced. Unhappily for such simple theories, individuals and groups engage in recurrent practices which are deeply rooted and which are often founded on pre-existing values and attitudes, as

this book has argued. People are not empty-headed, so easily swayed and influenced. Indeed, their practices, values and attitudes are often lent solidity from social structures outside the university in which they work: pressure groups, academic bodies, churches, charities, and so on. Universities as organisations are highly porous and so the power of their managers to change cultural characteristics is further reduced. (I have discussed these issues in more detail elsewhere: see Trowler, 1998, pp. 150–155.)

2. Dissatisfied with the limiting, static, and 'catch-all' characteristics of that approach, together with the way in which it tends to suggest that 'strong' cultures are deemed better and more functional than weaker ones, these critics have developed more ideographic approaches – ones which try to understand a particular organisation on its own terms. The example of Tierney's work (1988) was offered in Chapter 1. Tierney uses general headings to provide a unique but well-ordered description of Family State College which captures its distinctiveness yet could be used as the basis of comparison with other institutions. He acknowledges that in applying the concept of organisational culture in this way he has made no use of its subsets: subculture, anti-culture, or disciplinary culture. This is an important point: the concept of 'culture' used here, like the nomothetic approach, tends to conceive it as unitary and, in a sense, 'official'. The categories employed tend to capture 'corporate culture' – in other words, power relations, decision-making procedures, lines of information flow, corporate strategy, and the rest. It is less successful at capturing culture in a more sociological sense: relatively organised sets of assumptions, values, and attitudes; unreflective recurrent practices; taken-for-granted knowledge as well as discursive repertoires which permeate (or, rather, *constitute*) everyday life.

3. The phenomenological approach is also ideographic in the sense of offering unique pictures of organisations. However, it adopts a more intuitive approach in which the analyst arrives at an empathetic understanding of the nature of the culture at a particular site through experiencing it and then attempts to describe and analyse it. Kempner's (1991) study of Hill College is an example of this. It describes in graphic and fascinating detail a low-status higher education institution (HEI) in the United States. Such ideographic approaches yield rich, but unique, depictions of institutions. This uniqueness can make comparative analysis very difficult and so diminishes the value of the accounts for both the analyst and the decision-maker. So while the nomothetic approach lacks the fine-grained character and descriptive detail of the phenomenological one, it

offers an ability to make comparisons and high-level generalisations. In the final chapter I briefly discuss the tension between what is offered by the more nuanced but complex approaches in studies like Kempner's and the analytical simplicity offered approaches such as McNay's, which can lack descriptive detail.

4. The fourth approach, derived from the work of Alvesson (2002), sees universities as having a multiple cultural configuration. In this view it is always necessary to talk about organisational cultures in the plural, even for just one organisation. If, as the first part of the book argues, departmental and sub-departmental workgroups develop their own social worlds, sets of meanings (albeit sometimes multiple and conflicting), and unique recurrent practices, theories, discursive repertoires, and codes of signification, then essentially there will be multiple and diverse 'cultures' dynamically interacting within an organisational context. Of course, they will be nested within broader sets of understanding and practices, and will be dynamic and porous. Another way of putting this is to say that universities consist of multiple open, natural systems. Or, to use Alvesson's metaphor, they are like rivers with multiple streams flowing in complex ways. Tributaries run into the main river and change its character. Obstacles in the stream (a metaphor for contentious issues which expose alternative ways of seeing) throw up spray and expose to some extent the character of the flow. The flow of meaning from one culture to another is not seen as a transportation of a fixed unit of meaning that may be identified in its original form within the new context. Rather, flow manifests itself in new creations of meaning within the context of the receiving culture. (Svensson, 1998, p. 124). Hannerz (1992, p. 4) points out that the concept of flow is a little treacherous in that it suggests unimpeded transportation rather than the infinite and problematic occurrence of transformation. But cultures are like rivers in the sense that they seem permanent and highly structured, yet the structure is dependent upon an ongoing process: you cannot step into the same river twice. Moreover, a river changes its flow over time; it may even dry up or perhaps burst its banks.

▶ Vignette: An English department gets reviewed (derived from observant participation)

An English department in a British university founded in the 1960s underwent a quality review. The reviewers noticed that there was a strong collegial culture which extended from professors right through to undergraduate students. The department was not homogeneous, though – medievalists and creative writing staff had joined the department from elsewhere over time. Gradually, however, they had become integrated into the department, though their particular identities were still apparent and important, and defended by them. Staff were very willing to give time to seeing students and marking their work. Students loved the department and gradually came to understand how to do well there. The curriculum was quite traditional, with critical theory emphasised much less than in departments elsewhere and a traditional offering of 'the canon' rather more. Staff in the main taught about their research interests in the second and third years – the curriculum was organised around these. Senior staff, especially professors, were able to control their teaching much more than others, particularly in terms of time allocated and content.

Teaching assistants (TAs) were responsible for teaching first years – and while the TAs were fully involved in the collegial culture of the department, they clearly formed an identifiable subgroup within it. Assessment was largely by essay and exam, except in the first year, where the TAs had introduced more innovative assessment (and teaching) methods. Notions of peer-assessment or self-assessment by students were treated with mirth. Permanent staff believed that useful formative and summative feedback could only be provided by detailed feedback on essays, written after compulsory exposure to lectures and seminars. There was antipathy to writing and using marking criteria or indicators. The very general ones that existed were not much used. A common view was that two-dimensional articulations of practice like assessment criteria stood in the same relationship to practice as a stock cube does to a cow. They were seen, in other words, as damagingly reductionist.

Because of the approaches to teaching and learning adopted here, including the lack of explicit articulation of assessment criteria, students had to 'feel' their way into an understanding of the prerequisites for success. The close attention that staff gave them helped them to do this. While being collegial and warm, this system was dependent on individual members of staff being present and able to give time to students. The courses too were tied very closely to individual members of staff. Developments in higher education such as massification and new quality regimes also made the department highly vulnerable to risk. Moreover, all staff felt that the assessment 'load' was an excessive burden but were unwilling to consider innovative ways to 'do more with less', as they were being urged to by the university. Instead, they pointed out that they had been required to do more (of the same) with fewer and fewer resources for many years. They took it for granted that doing more of the same in changing circumstances was the most principled option to take.

► **Commentary**

This vignette offers an example of a TLR in one department in one university. Apparent here are, for example, power relations (between the professors and the more junior members of staff); implicit theories of teaching and learning (the socialisation of students into the discipline); discursive repertoires (in, for example, the phrase 'teaching load' and the metaphors used); conventions of appropriateness (in relation to peer-assessment, for example); and recurrent practices (in terms of teaching approaches taken).

This one department, itself divided in many ways, forms part of a much wider and even more complex multiple cultural configuration in this university. Clearly, an initiative to do with student self-assessment or designed to alter teaching and learning practices to make them more efficient will 'hit' this department in particular ways, being received, understood, reinterpreted, and implemented in quite specific ways. Other departments, while part of the same institution, will look quite different and respond differently. This multiple cultural configuration makes life difficult for the top team charged with implementing broad policy initiatives *across* the university.

As well as having multiple cultures, though, the picture is further complicated by the fact that universities are playing multiple 'games' at the same time (Lucas, 2006). These games have different rules, different goals, and different rewards and sanctions for winning or losing. So, for example, in the United Kingdom universities are engaged in the 'research game', aiming to enhance their research output, impact, and esteem in return for private and public funding. This itself is divided into various sub-games: the game of reputation and resources; the game of publications and priorities, and so on (Lucas, 2006). At the same time they are playing the 'teaching game', aiming to improve their league table positions as well as students' satisfaction and QAA scores, though usually for little direct financial return. They are also chasing, funding, and trying to widen participation as well as responding to other government and client demands. Needless to say, these games are not necessarily mutually compatible: investing effort to win at one may well be at the cost of another. Though universities frequently claim that their teaching and learning is enhanced by their work on research, the evidence on this is mixed, and there is some evidence from students that the research effort can even be deleterious to their experience (Lindsay et al., 2002).

Individuals and committees in universities usually cope with this diversity in game-playing by concentrating on only one game at any one time, in effect by wearing blinkers. This can lead to decisions which, while sensible in relation to one game, make no sense at all in relation to another. The significance of this culturally is that lines of consensus and conflict shift as the agenda, or game, shifts from one to another: the picture we draw of cultures depends to some extent on the issues at hand.

▶ Learning organisations, learning architectures, and enhancement cultures

As we have just seen, conceptualising universities as having a dynamic multiple cultural configuration creates problems for managers responsible for bringing about change. Rather than seeing the university as having a single character upon which innovations can be impressed, the picture becomes an altogether more complex one. The same proposals for change will be received, understood, and implemented in different ways in different parts of the university and so expected outcomes will be highly diverse. This in fact is the experience of most university leaders at institutional and faculty level as well as one of the findings of studies of change more generally.

Three things can assist in the change process at the organisational level. First, moving the university in the direction of becoming a 'learning organisation', that is one that is responsive to past events. Second, and associated with this, developing a 'learning architecture', that is a series of structures, systems, and processes which together assist the university in improving its performance in different areas of activity on the basis of reflection on past and current practices and taking action based on that. Third, and finally, it needs to develop enhancement cultures at the departmental level, encouraging departments to be reflective and to develop their practices in desirable ways, but ones which are appropriate for them. Next I deal with these three characteristics.

Learning organisations

The organisational context of enhancement efforts can impede or facilitate changes. This section considers the characteristics of universities as learning organisations, ones that are responsive to past events and change their practices as a result.

Clearly, universities need to be learning organisations which become aware of problems and try as far as possible to 'join up' what they do. One of the key characteristics of 'learning organisations' according to the relevant literature is that they are open to organisational learning, which means that

a) They openly reflect on themselves and past problems and practices which have led to less than optimal outcomes. This reflective process can become ossified into routines undergone as part of the quality assurance practices of a university. Political considerations about audiences and image can interfere with genuine reflection, as can the temptations of saving time through turning the process into a formal box-ticking exercise to satisfy bureaucratic requirements.

b) They are open to new practices, new theories, new discourses, and new ideas about what is and is not appropriate. They are ready to question their own assumptions. Again, the danger here is parochialism and complacency, combined with the fact that re-thinking practices and approaches requires time and effort. This is not an attractive proposition in an environment where work is being intensified.

c) Their openness is directed towards enhancement in their key functions, especially (for our purposes) the enhancement of teaching and learning. Again, the multiple 'games' that universities play means that it is sometimes hard to keep a focus on one thing for very long: priorities can shift because of environmental factors such as the latest research assessment exercise or the publication of a league table.

d) There is effective and wide-ranging dissemination of ideas about improved practices and approaches across the institution. Ideally this will lead to implementation of improved ways of doing things, albeit in different ways in the different contexts of the organisation.

e) Learning organisations also have good organisational memories (Huber, 1991). Organisational memory is found in multiple dimensions of its practices, paperwork, routines, and so on. Remembering things that worked, remembering mistakes, and remembering the stage reached in processes (and what needs to be done next) is important in terms of both efficiency and improvement. So is the fact that the remembering is organisational, not just located in the heads of individuals who may move on. The vignette below elaborates on this point.

Learning organisations also need to square the circle of acknowledging (and seeing as a strength) internal diversity while achieving high standards across the organisation. Often the halo effect of a few excellent departments means that the less-than-optimal practices, attitudes, theories, and assumptions found in others are ignored. Such departments benefit from the reflected glory of their more effective equivalents elsewhere in the university.

So, for those members of the top team charged with improving teaching and learning in their universities, the important questions are as follows:

1. Does my university have the capacity to understand any deficiencies it has or errors that have been made? (Do those responsible for quality assurance identify these in a systematic way or do they, rather, simply ensure compliance with the relevant official requirements in terms of paperwork and processes?)
2. In what ways does my university open itself to new ideas and alternative ways of doing things? (When it becomes aware of issues to be resolved does it invent solutions on the fly or does it systematically scan the environment to consider responses and solutions from elsewhere?) Do its internal procedures encourage and value good quality messages from outside?
3. When alternative ways of doing things are proposed, is careful and thorough thought given to implementation processes so that real changes are made to practices across the university? (Or is there a tacit view that policy-making is enough?)
4. Is careful thought given to the extent of change across the university and its sustainability? (Or is it enough to see success in some parts of the university and amongst some individuals there – the enthusiastic 'usual suspects' trapped in ghettos?)

▶ Vignette: How a cockpit remembers its speeds: Representations and processes outside the pilots (adapted from Hutchins, 1995b)

The distributed nature of organisational memory is illustrated in the way appropriate and safe speeds at different points in the flight of a commercial aircraft are determined and remembered not only by the pilots but by the cockpit itself (Hutchins, 1995b). The correct speed for a particular aeroplane at the various points in its journey is never a constant but is conditional on a number of factors: the weight of its load, wind speed, the length of the runway, the configuration of the flight surfaces of the plane, as well as other factors. Thus for each journey it is necessary to determine and remember right speeds at which, for example, take-off can be aborted, at which the wheels should leave the ground, at which manoeuvering can take place, at which the aircraft will stall in flight, at which the approach to the destination airport should take place, and the correct and safe speed for landing.

Clearly, a lot of this happens through the intelligence of the pilots, but this determination and memory of speeds is also distributed around the cockpit. The pilots refer to a 'speed card' for the particular plane they are flying, which sets out in tabular form limitations on its speeds for particular weights. In a sense this is the long-term memory in the cockpit system. There are physical 'bugs', coloured pointers around the edge of the speed dial, and the pilots change their position for each flight, marking relevant speeds for particular flight phases. These bugs represent part of the short-term memory outside of the pilots. They not only record the appropriate speeds, but do so in a way which objectifies those speeds and situates them in relation to other information: the speed indicator needle. This would not happen if that dimension of memory was simply in a pilot's head or written down, making the task more difficult and potentially more error-prone. The amount of cognitive labour is thus reduced. Warning systems add to the distributed memory of the cockpit: they represent a form of latent memory, reminding the pilots that they have allowed the plane to fly too fast or too low in certain conditions.

What is happening here is that the pilots are manipulating and interpreting physical and other symbolic forms rather than only drawing on their own memories and cognitive processes directly. They are facilitated in this by a set of routines, recurrent practices, set out in flying manuals, which tell them what to do and what to say to each other in what order. These routine practices too are part of the cockpit's memory.

▶ Commentary

The point of this vignette is to show that remembering and knowledge are not necessarily just located in the individual, in the head of the pilot, but can be a process, a socio-technical system. Knowledge and memory are seen as essentially *distributed* here, with organisational knowledge located in different parts of that system which works smoothly and very consistently regardless of the characteristics of particular pilots. Nowadays computers do a lot of this.

While flying a plane might seem to have little to do with higher education, the same can be true of the processes in that context too. Administrators and academics very often carry crucial organisational information in their heads, but systemically the system is safer, and more able to learn when organisational memory and knowledge are distributed across different types of locale, not just in the heads of its members. The next vignette amplifies this point, this time in a higher education context.

▶ Vignette: Distributed cognition and the domestication of quality processes (adapted from Trowler *et al.*, 2002)

A department realised that its teaching would not rate highly in terms of the formal procedures expected by the quality assurance agency. There would be a QAA inspection in the next two or three years. Changes would have to be made. Academics, though, saw their modules as their fiefs and most could mount an epistemological critique of the QAA approach to teaching improvement.

The undergraduate programme leader concentrated on domesticating QAA requirements to be compatible with departmental values. Three examples follow: programme specification in terms of skills to be acquired, criteria-referenced assessment, and the development of a new undergraduate programme.

Few people in the department believed in 'skills'. One professor would mount a critique that cited Wittgenstein's position on rules and the psychology of situated cognition. However, they accepted that what they did and valued could be described in the language of skills. Those people who believed in skills could describe departmental practices in the skills language.

Brief descriptions of what students tend to learn in this sort of degree were circulated to academics who were asked to identify any that could be strongly associated with their modules and to add any that were missed. With some creative editing, a draft list of the sorts of learning stimulated by the programme was produced, along with a grid showing what was being promoted where. It was discussed, 'tuned', and then checked in two ways. First, colleagues were asked to identify the teaching and learning practices they used to promote the learning they said was central to their modules. Second, they completed another grid showing how they assessed this learning. (The assessment task was supported by a note explaining that assessment could be formative or summative and that outcomes could be directly and singly assessed, assessed as a group, or caught up in the assessment of other learning. This 'tool' was essential.) More deliberation and tuning followed. Academics then re-presented their modules' learning goals in terms of the programme specification, which, with some final tuning, was then formally accepted. It was complemented by three charts showing which outcomes were being emphasised in which courses, the methods used to do so, and the associated assessment arrangements. These tools helped the team improve programme coherence and progression and highlighted areas to be emphasised in new module developments.

126 Cultures and Change in Higher Education

These academics were also hostile to the use of criteria in essay marking but external examiners and QAA expectations made them grudgingly accept that there needed to be some, although there were those who argued that criteria could never displace judgement. The idea of grade indicators or 'fuzzy' criteria was acceptable. Draft indicators were presented, revised, discussed with external examiners, tried, revised, and stabilised. This is another example, then, of change being effected through tool development.

But then neither educators nor students proved to be too scrupulous about using them. This was addressed by printing the standard essay criteria on all the cover/feedback sheets that students attached to each essay; inviting them to say which criteria best described their work; stating that feedback should be in terms of criteria, both when it came to explaining the mark awarded and making suggestions for improvement; and getting the second marker to verify that the criteria had been used appropriately. A simple change of stationery – a new cover/feedback sheet – got grade indicators into common use.

An opportunity arose to develop a brand new undergraduate programme. Colleagues found that ideas which had been unvalidatable a year before could now be convincingly presented with the help of tools like the programme specification (customised to the new degree) and grade indicators (likewise extended).

The department scored full marks in the QAA review and received a glowing oral report.

▶ **Commentary**

There are two significant points about this vignette:

First, the changes were made not only by making changes to the practices and attitudes of the staff involved but by making changes to the systems in which they operated. New tools were developed and changes were made to those that had been in place already. In this way this vignette illustrates the nature of distributed cognition within organisations, a concept introduced in the vignette about how a cockpit remembers its speeds.

The second point is that the changes made in this department did not involve slavishly following the QAA requirements. Rather the department adapted its practices in appropriate ways. This process of adaptation rather than adoption almost always happens because changes occur within previously existing situations. This is the process of 'domestication'. In this case the adaptation was done in an 'administrative' way, with formal changes being made. Sometimes the process of domestication is informal and unacknowledged, especially where there is fear that rules are being broken or stretched.

Learning architectures

The 'architectural' characteristics of a learning organisation refers to the structures and processes that enable it to become and remain effective at learning and implementing change as a result. This includes committee structures (to do with quality assurance, with teaching, and with research, for example), the nature of sub-units and their responsibilities, lines of reporting, and the ways decisions are arrived at.

David Dill (1999) explores the characteristics of learning architectures and shows how they might enable an institution to develop and transfer knowledge for the improvement of its own basic processes. A good learning architecture should help an institution give affirmative answers to the four questions above (p. 123), offering robust systems and structures which give organisational learning sustainability. When in place it should allow the institution to identify errors and problems as well as solve them: it will help the institution to learn from its own experience as well as learning from others, it will facilitate experimentation with new approaches and the transfer of knowledge, and finally it will enable the institution to measure its own learning and the progress it has made.

On the basis of his empirical research in American universities Dill recommends the use of systematic evaluations. University-wide centres for teaching and learning can offer ways in which experiences can be analysed, evaluated, and act as a basis for proposals for change. According to Dill, the development or evolution of pan-university structures for providing more effective coordination, support, and accountability of the systematic improvement of teaching and learning is very significant. In the United Kingdom, though, such teaching and learning centres tend not to do such evaluations, while quality support offices tend to be focused on complying with external demands, particularly those of the QAA. The practice of external benchmarking can help institutions consider alternative ways of doing things when evaluations show there are difficulties. The use of external reviewers, study tours, and other methods to learn from others is particularly important in university contexts. Dill talks about *adopting* successful processes from other organisations, but there are problems with this transfer model: adaptation rather than adoption is likely to be the watchword. Earlier in the book I have argued that the process of domestication is important, but that does not mean that the experience of others is insignificant in new contexts. On the contrary, experience and practices elsewhere can be taken and remade in very effective ways.

Biggs (2001) makes the point that sometimes we need to look again at practices we tend to take for granted when we look for opportunities to improve organisational learning. Reframing the external examiner role to becoming a 'consultant' for example, or looking again at how validation panels do their work and what their remit is. Similarly, some practices may have unintended negative consequences and need to be reviewed or even terminated: the effect of awards to 'distinguished teachers' on 'undistinguished' ones (everyone else) is one example Biggs cites. Other authors, for example, Patterson et al. (2002) and Seel (2000), stress the significance of intra-organisational discussions in organisational learning and reflecting on local practices and attitudes.

Discussions with key 'stakeholders', analogous providers in other locations and situations, and with students are another way of developing new knowledge to improve and develop core processes. As the power of disciplines has shifted in the direction of new reference groups such as 'professions, vocations, industry and community groups' (Becher and Parry, 2005, p. 139) in the search for new sources of income, it has become increasingly important to do this. Universities can be parochial, unable to learn lessons from elsewhere, or even sometimes resistant to trying. Evaluative work and careful thinking about the points of view of non-academics can offer insights into alternative ways of doing things. However, new knowledge can be developed not only through collecting evidence about one's own experiences and borrowing from others but also through carefully designed 'experiments' or projects with new tools or processes. This happens in many universities, especially where funding is available for experimentation and pilot projects. However, as even a cursory glance at some of the journals on learning technologies shows, many funded 'solutions' never go further than their originators, disappearing into the black hole labelled *no implementation plan*. As McInnis (2005, pp. 87–88) points out, 'Even large-scale, well-funded innovations such as the [UK's] "Teaching and Learning Technology Programme" failed to make a sustainable impact', largely because of the, absence of a plan for wider application.

The tough part is scaling up, moving from the localised or pilot phase to wider use. Here the problem relates to learning the lessons from the experiments, admitting and carefully analysing weaknesses and failure, as well as communicating ideas for success more widely. Too often there is ghettoisation and, once the funding has gone, the project dies.

Thus an important aspect of learning architecture is the development of structures which support and sustain innovation over extended periods. Likewise, Dill notes that there is a need for improved communication between teaching departments, or between innovative units and the broader organisation. Too often pockets of innovation remain relatively autonomous, thus losing the valuable organisational capability of the integration of specialist knowledge and learning from one another. Even something as simple as geographical location can be important in this. Some of the 74 Centres for Excellence in Teaching and Learning, set up and developed in the first decade of the 21st century and situated within universities in the United Kingdom, developed such things as innovative learning spaces. But often these were so physically isolated from the rest of the university that a deliberate effort was needed to encounter them.

Dill's advice to universities to measure their own learning involves developing indicators of organisational performance which can then be used to evaluate whether organisational learning is actually occurring. It is ironic that universities should need to learn to use evidence properly in enhancing their own practices, given that the use of an evidence base is part of the daily life of disciplines. And yet it is clearly a requirement of a good learning architecture, and is often missing. Intra-organisational communication of knowledge is best achieved in contexts that

1. provide meaningful performance measures;
2. provide incentives to improve performance;
3. give legitimacy to performance improvement through the adaptation of successful practices from other units;
4. facilitate the development of new knowledge and ultimately its transfer.

In contrast, an organisational context that neither encourages organisational units to develop their learning capacities nor fosters close relationships among them will, in the end, not involve organisational learning.

▶ Vignette: The Common Curriculum: Exposing the currents in the stream (*Source*: data collected by the author in South Africa)

This vignette draws on data collected in the South African context described on p. viii. As recounted there, this new South African university was created as a result of the merger of four smaller institutions. These had been very different in size, resources, student body, and historical background. Two of the larger sites contrasted particularly starkly. One had historically been a disadvantaged and predominantly black university, the other historically a white very advantaged university. The senior management team of the merged university had instructed the now-merged (but previously separate) subject departments, teaching on different campuses, to adopt common subject content – a 'common curriculum' – though that team had not specified exactly what they meant by that term.

For example, lawyers on one campus had to negotiate a common curriculum with lawyers on another, even though both had sometimes been teaching somewhat different subjects in quite different ways in very different contexts. The same applied to all the other disciplines taught on two or more campuses of this newly merged university. This involved a series of meetings and much e-mail communication. Of course, it also involved bargaining, a lot of emotion, and quite a bit of mutual recrimination. The vagueness of the concept of 'common curriculum' led to different views on how much commonality was required, and in what areas.

This process, though, led each department involved in the negotiations to look at its practices, sets of assumptions, and conventions of appropriateness in new ways. In effect, the forced comparison with another department in the same subject represented a mirror on their own practices. The example given earlier (p. 94) concerning the different uses made of GTAs provides an example of this.

▶ **Commentary**

Had the merger and the quest for the common curriculum not required this department to look elsewhere, their practices in relation to the use of GTAs would not have become 'de-normalised' in this way. This example shows how events such as this can be a catalyst for reflection and, in the right circumstances, change. In the case study in question, however, what tended to happen was a struggle between cognate departments to impose *their* way of doing things. In the absence of appropriate top-down direction power struggles at the meso level tended to dominate outcomes.

___

Enhancement cultures

However, restructuring the university and developing a sophisticated, communicative, learning architecture is not in itself enough to ensure that enhancement initiatives come to fruition. As the second quote at the head of this chapter suggests, the departmental context is often the rock on which initiatives founder and adapting university structures is in itself not enough to bring about a readiness to develop appropriately. So, in addition to developing an institutional learning architecture, there needs to be underpinning enhancement cultures located at the departmental level. The key characteristic of this is reflexivity, an ability to combine reflection with action. I have argued elsewhere (Trowler et al., 2005, p. 441) that a reflexive department is one which

- is self-conscious about the nature of its TLR – has surfaced its previously implicit theories, developed consciousness about its recurrent practices, and has a greater awareness generally about the specific character of the components of its TLR;
- collectively evaluates how it operates as a department, and how its particular regime influences this, and works to bring about change for the better;
- then actually makes changes in its practices in such a way as to enhance learning and teaching or to make that enhancement more likely.

The key question, however, is, how to bring this about? 'Culturalism' (that is the notion that cultures in organisations can be consciously manipulated by managers) is fashionable amongst some authors, for example, Peters and Waterman (1982) and nowadays Wenger (2000, and Wenger et al., 2002). However, other authors (Willmott, 1993; Parker, 2000) have cautioned against the notion that cultural manipulation using management levers is easy or even possible, and not desirable either. Moreover, while it is easy to advise departments to reflect on their own practices prior to changing them, being able to convert good advice into action on the ground is trickier. Why should departments suddenly give priority to spending time reflecting on their current practices, attitudes, and assumptions? And even if they do, how can the outcomes be converted into sustainable change, new policies with real impact?

Furthermore, useful reflection on the current nature of a particular department and its practices cannot happen without a good understanding of the nature of academic departments. Implicit theories about the nature of departments are often revealed in the advice given to them. For example, Jenkins and Zetter (2003, p. 18) suggest departments address the following questions to help them define research-informed teaching:

- What is your departmental (and disciplinary) understanding or conception of research-based or informed learning?
- What forms of pedagogy and their assessment do you consider appropriate to support these conceptions?

The problems here include the following:

- the assumption of a unitary understanding of research-informed teaching across the department;
- that assumptions can be easily surfaced simply by asking the question;
- that practices (forms of pedagogy and their assessment) are directly related to those understandings;
- that statements about understandings and practices reflect *actual* understandings and practices;
- and that the process of uncovering understandings and practices in this way is a neutral one, not influenced by political and other considerations affecting those engaged in it.

This is not to say that groups within organisations cannot become more aware of their own characteristics, only that this does not tend to happen in normal times. Much as fish are perhaps unaware of the water in which they swim, cultural contexts become 'normalised' for those who inhabit them (Trowler and Knight, 2000) and there are always more pressing priorities for departments than looking in the mirror. However, circumstances can offer more organic opportunities for reflection, and the top team, institutional policies, or national ones can create the circumstances in which such opportunities arise.

The key point, as noted above, is to have in place a learning architecture which takes advantage of such opportunities. What these opportunities are might vary from place to place and time to time, but they might include the following:

- the need to prepare for quality audit;
- a department's need to face a crisis such as the decline in the number of undergraduate students;
- the decision to redesign the programme or introduce a new one;
- a sudden decline in funding;
- a sudden increase in the number of students to be taught;
- a sudden turnover in staffing as a large cohort reaches retirement age;
- annual programme reviews and assessment boards.

The top team and institutional policies can provide the framework which encourages departments to think more broadly when such opportunities arise, giving them appropriate tools for the development of learning as well as the space, legitimacy, power, and confidence to explore their practices and reframe them as necessary (Boreham and Morgan, 2004), as well as sharing their conclusions, decisions, and reasons with others in the institution and beyond it.

▶ Conclusion

The organisational shape of universities and the ways in which practices, policies, and procedures are organised and intersect are vitally important for effectiveness in carrying out tasks and in introducing new, perhaps better, ways of doing things, or new things to do. This chapter has suggested ways in which organisational structures may be viewed at in order to make enhancement more likely.

However, I think it is necessary to end this chapter with a note of caution. Like many books and articles in this field, the chapter has treated organisations as if they were neutral sets of arrangements divorced from the cut and thrust of life at work. The approach has been a technical-rational one rather than one rooted in issues of power, identities, legacies from the past, personal ambitions, and a rapidly changing environment. The eight moments of the teaching and learning regimes, discussed earlier, attempt to bring these dimensions back into an understanding of organisational life. They should not be forgotten in discussions of organisational culture and organisational design.

In discussing the changing nature of organisational structures in universities in the United Kingdom John Taylor (2006) points out that changing structures involve changes in power relations and changes in academic identities, changes which involve the surrender of academic supremacy in directing their institutions to the forward march of managerialism. Similarly, Craig McInnis (2005), commenting on Kogan's work, notes how organisational change in universities has been part of the shift in power away from academics in departments towards the faculty level and institutional leadership as well as, indirectly, to state power and to the 'market'. As institutions seek to respond to an increasingly turbulent, marketised, and 'supercomplex' environment, there are internal shifts in power relations and identities. At the same time the significance of disciplines as organising structures has diminished (Becher and Parry, 2005). Sometimes such changes are negotiated or contested, sometimes not. For many the debates and decisions about organisational structures and governance can seem a long way from the day-to-day concerns of teaching, learning, research, and administration. Yet the resultant structures have implications for years to come for academics, for students, and for the nature of universities themselves.

6 Enhancing Teaching and Learning

Men [and women] make their own history, but they do not make it as they please; they do not make it under self-selected circumstances, but under circumstances existing already, given and transmitted from the past.

(Marx, 1852)

Teachers and students do not merely receive and 'act out' externally imposed prescriptions of their tasks, they 'act upon' those prescriptions in the construction of their own practices. They are actors, acting in accordance with their own understandings and constructions and it is precisely for this reason that programmes to change, if they are to have any effect, must be directed to those understandings and constructions.

(Bloomer, 1997, pp. 186–197)

How can the lessons of these ... case studies be adapted to the dissemination of [other teaching and learning innovations]? ... the answer would appear to be simple: choose a topic for dissemination which fits in well with the academic culture of the targeted group

(Elton, 2002, p. 12)

Some innovations seem to die on contact with ... institutional reality ... It is a rare reform that performs and persists precisely according to plan. Even long-lasting reforms are not static but evolve in ways often not foreseen by their proponents.

(Tyack and Cuban, 1995, p. 60)

This chapter has two sections, each informed by the discussion in the foregoing chapters. The first addresses the question 'what makes teaching and learning enhancement initiatives likely to succeed?' The second asks what we should expect when we try to enhance teaching and learning.

▶ **What makes teaching and learning enhancement initiatives likely to succeed?**

In thinking about the likely success of an enhancement initiative it is useful to consider the nature of the initiative itself, the character of teaching and learning regimes locally, and how the two elements interact with each other.

Examples of initiatives could include a new application of information technology for learning, a new teaching and learning policy, a particular technique to be adopted, or compliance to new requirements in programme design. Here key questions include the following:

Where does it come from? An initiative from a generally disliked quality assurance body is obviously a problem. One from the institution's top team might be received better, depending on the climate in the institution. One from an enthusiast within a department is likely to get local implementation, but the problem of scaling up from that will be significant. An initiative that results from an internal quality review will have a chance of success if everyone agrees that the problem has been correctly identified and is significant. Whatever the answer to this question is, it will give a clue as to how the initiative will be 'read' on the ground, and so whether likely responses are going to be resistive, adaptive, or ready adoption. Naturally, a detailed understanding of how an initiative is likely to read and implemented will require detailed knowledge of both the initiative itself and the context of its application. But considering *where* the initiative comes from is a significant first step.

How well resourced is the initiative, and how seriously is it being pursued? Clearly, an initiative needs adequate funds in place to see it through. And the period of funding needs to be long enough to make the development sustainable. Prioritisation is significant: sometimes, initiatives fail because other issues take precedence as circumstances change, especially where funding is tight and conditional. However, inappropriate resourcing can also skew initiatives in particular ways. This may happen where priorities are set centrally but do not address the real needs on the ground (as occurred in Operation Blackboard, pp. 39–40) or where money is thrown at a problem without clarity of thought about how best to use it to solve that problem. These are obvious points, but the resources which underpin initiatives as well as the sustainability issue are ones which recur in the analysis of failed innovations. Often staff are expected to add a new development to an already crowded portfolio of tasks and responsibilities, funds are not adequate to see through all necessary aspects of a project, and the time-limited nature of project funds can mean that the priorities of staff involved begin to drift even before completion.

What codes of signification does the initiative carry? An innovation itself may carry meanings which help or hinder the implementation process, and the discursive repertoires used in introducing it may resonate with or alienate those on the ground. Emotional loading is very significant, though to fully appreciate its potential effects in particular contexts requires an intimate knowledge of those contexts. But even without this reflection on likely gut responses to initiatives at the local level is valuable for those keen to implement change.

How will it affect existing power relations? Here the question concerns who are the likely winners and who the losers if the innovation were to be adopted. There are almost always winners and losers (at least subjectively) in any change in arrangements. Whether the change concerns organisational structure, curricular change, or a change in practices of teaching and learning, the power structure will shift in one way or another. For academics a significant issue is the relative autonomy they have over their working lives (Halsey, 1992). Innovations and developments which threaten this (and many do) can be received very negatively unless they offer other attractions, or save time in other areas.

How will it affect existing subjectivities? Individual identities and the patterns of interaction between them in the social context are sometimes changed, threatened, or enhanced (in terms, for example, of self-esteem) as social practices change. Practices involve the articulation of personal identity, or subjectivity: 'the expert', 'the facilitator', 'the counsellor', and so on. New practices sometimes involve, or threaten, a change to an individual's persona, to their view of themselves, and to the way they think others see them. This may enhance or limit the chances of successful implementation.

What theory of change underpins the initiative? Here the question is about the assumptions (often tacit) about how an initiative is expected to change practices in the longer term. Often initiatives are undertaken with only a vague idea of how they may lead to broader change. An evaluation of the National Teaching Fellowship Scheme in the United Kingdom identified the lack of a good theory of change underpinning it as a serious problem: how would rewarding 50 good teachers with a lot of money to undertake a 3-year project bring about broader systemic change (Skelton, 2004)? A clearly thought-through theory of change is likely to be more helpful than vague notions of 'motivational beacons' or 'contagion'.

In thinking about the context of implementation it is helpful to consider existing patterns of the eight moments as well as the levels and patterns of diversity and consensus within regimes. Here key questions include the following:

How do discursive repertoires in use relate to the discursive framing of the initiative? The vignette on pp. 78–80 concerning 'the new route PhD' illustrates the negative effect of jarring discursive repertoires.

What is the disposition of power relations and will this be affected by the initiative? An example is the introduction of student self- and peer-assessment. This has the potential to make fundamental changes in the balance of power between students and their teachers.

What kinds of subjectivities are in place and how do they interact? Initiatives that attempt to replace the didactic 'sage on the stage' with the facilitative 'guide at the side' have immense significance for academic and student identities, for example.

What are the dominant implicit theories of teaching and learning in place? The vignette about Operation Blackboard on pp. 39–40 demonstrates contrasting theories of teaching and learning can lead to an initiative getting stuck.

What sets of recurrent practices are in place? Initiatives always involve a change in practices, and new practices are rarely completely new but are grafted onto existing patterns of behaviour. So the question here is about the relationship between practices in place and proposed new ones.

What sets of conventions of appropriateness are in place? Here the question relates to any potential contravention of what is considered appropriate, 'normal', in a given situation, and the nature and extent of that. Associated with this are the codes of signification that might be mobilised by any proposed change in practices.

Finally, how do the tacit assumptions on the ground relate to those at work in the minds of those who planned the initiative? (Again, Operation Blackboard on pp. 39–40 demonstrates significant differences in this regard.)

In addition to the characteristics *currently* in place, narratives about the *history* of local contexts are also significant in the reception and implementation of change strategies. Earlier I used the shorthand term 'the backstory' to describe this – it usually involves multiple lines of narrative so that any enhancement initiative that is introduced will relate in different ways to those different lines and will be an insertion and a particular point historically. How people in workgroups view their own history and that of their institution, the stories they tell, impinges very directly on how they receive and implement proposals for change. There may be congruence between the backstory and the new initiative, or there may not. For example, there may be a narrated history of failure or success in the area of the initiative, and agendas and concepts may be mobilised to support or reject it. Thinking in terms of the verb 'changing' rather than the more static noun 'change' helps to historically situate an initiative.

So, in considering the nature and the interaction between initiative and context, issues of salience, congruence between them as well as profitability for those involved are absolutely central. Salience refers to the significance of an initiative in a particular context, the extent to which it addresses felt needs, interests, and agendas. Congruence relates to the extent to which an initiative matches discourses, theories, practices, and other dimensions of 'culture'; in other words, to the degree of fit between a teaching and learning regime on the one hand and the characteristics of an enhancement initiative on the other. Profitability (Levine, 1980) refers to the degree of perceived benefit inherent in an enhancement initiative for individuals and groups. Where there is salience, congruence, and profitability, the chances of success are high. In academic life the most important dimension of profitability is often to do with time, especially freeing time for busy academics.

An example to illustrate these points is the provision of development courses and teaching qualifications for academics. Åkerlind (2007) makes the point that academics as teachers have different approaches to teaching and different sets of concerns in relation to change and development. They may see development in terms of developing knowledge of their content area, on gaining experience in how to teach, in developing a repertoire of teaching strategies to become more skilful and more effective, or in developing understanding to become more effective in facilitating student learning. The provision of courses and qualifications may be based on strategies which are congruent or not with the approach adopted by the individual. If they are not then the content will not be salient for that person:

> It is only when academics' understanding of teaching development comes to include the development of a repertoire of teaching strategies that they would be interested in educational development courses or workshops, and only when their understanding comes to include reflecting on what works and doesn't work in their teaching that the emphasis on reflective practice, including preparation of teaching portfolios, that is so common in educational development courses would be valued.
>
> (Åkerlind, 2007, p. 34)

Åkerlind concludes that to be effective development support must be tailored to individual academics' intentions and understandings with regard to teaching and teaching development. If it is not then the result will be that some academics will find such support valuable while others will not. One problem with Åkerlind's approach, though, lies in the focus on the individual which she adopts. While her analysis is pertinent, it does not address the question of the 'readiness' of the *department* in which the individual is located to support or sustain their developing approach to teaching. This level of analysis needs to be taken into account too when looking at the question of the effectiveness of educational development courses as a mechanism for the enhancement of teaching and learning at the institutional level. Ali Cooper and I attempted to do this in our 2002 paper (Trowler and Cooper, 2002), which also asked the question (as the editor put it) 'why such courses can be perceived as both "wonderful and crapulous" at the same time by different people?'

▶ Vignette: When teaching and learning regimes collide: Dealing with change in tricky situations (adapted from Fenwick, 2004)

Using critical discourse analysis of documents and 14 personal in-depth interviews, Fenwick studied a Canadian university laboratory centre (ULC) which delivered instruction to 350 children in primary school–level classes. It acted as a research site as well as a teaching centre. Its approach was student-centred, or progressive, involving parents as much as possible and a collaborative approach to teaching and curriculum design.

By 2000 the ULC school had outgrown its classroom spaces at the university and so the director approached the local city school district (CSD). The CSD identified a primary school near to the university, called Seaview School, as a possible new site for the ULC. Parents and ULC teachers as well as the ULC director and senior principal formed a partnership to which all parties were pledged. 'Eventually a partnership agreement was created and implemented, but not without stormy meetings, polarised positions, misunderstandings and the departure of the public-school [Seaview] principal on stress-related disability leave' (p. 175).

One of the main problems about this partnership was the different discursive repertoires found within it. 'City school district administrators and the university lab centre administrators each employed a distinctive language.... many of these educational administrators did not indicate awareness of these discursive dynamics...' (p. 176). The CSD discourse was managerial-structural in character. Partners were described as 'stakeholders', and the goal of a partnership was to achieve an 'administrative arrangement' that must be 'hammered out' in 'nitty-gritty details'. The partnership negotiations were portrayed in managerial terms: 'mediating highly intense emotions and commitments' and 'clarifying core values' (indicating that these could be articulated explicitly so that common values could be identified and agreed). This discourse assumed a clear centre of authority that legitimately exercises control over school programmes, personnel, determination of appropriate pedagogies, and so on.

By contrast, the discourse apparently shared among the directors, teachers, and parents of the ULC was informal, feelings-based, and could be characterised as fluid-communal. Thus, for example, while the CSD professionals talked of 'teachers' aides', the ULC group preferred to describe this role as 'teaching partners'. The different conceptions of power relations between the teacher and the person in this role is clear in the discourse used about it.

Across the two discursive groups the same terms were often used, but with very different meanings. 'Integrity' and 'core values' were powerful signifiers for both groups but meant very different things, carrying very different codes of signification for each of them. For the CSD administrators integrity was about commitment to the whole project, while for the ULC it was about preserving a small, special community and its freedom-in-enquiry teaching and learning approaches. 'Research' for ULC was longer-term basic scholarship, while for the CSD 'research' signified work that was short-term, applied, and related directly to the goals of the district such as improving schools' achievement.

The CSD discourse and the ULC discourse did not form two homogeneous blocs. There were discursive tensions within the each of these groups. For example, a ULC teacher bemoaned the lack of accountability and regulation, suggesting that 'teachers were getting away with anything'. This teacher felt that the ULC had started to lose its integrity, that teachers and the director had become self-interested, even selfish: 'it started to fall apart'. Eventually, this person resigned her post rather than pursue conflict and confrontation. However, the dominant fluid-communal discourse had been fragmented by her critique. On the other side, the new Seaview principal appeared in some ways more at home in the ULC language than in the managerial-structural discourse of the CSD. She claimed to be excited by the opportunity to learn about project-based pedagogy, which was aligned with her own teaching philosophies. However, new to the job, she felt uncomfortable expressing her natural alignment with the ULC philosophy and discourse. 'So she assumed that her natural instincts toward more personal one-to-one relationships were wrong, and strove to emulate the former principal's structural approaches' (p. 181).

In both these examples of internal discursive tensions the two individuals became aware of the conflict between the dominant discourse and their own desires and natural tendencies. One withdrew by resigning; the other adopted the dominant discourse. 'The appearance of shared understanding conceals multiple conflicting interactions as community

Table 6.1 Fenwick's account viewed in terms of teaching and learning regimes

Moments of Teaching and learning regimes	Fenwick's analysis considered in TLR terms-examples
Implicit theories of teaching and learning	Constructivist (ULC) Transmissive (CSD)
Conventions of appropriateness	Teacher is in charge (CSD) Egalitarian family-like relationships (ULC)
Recurrent practices	Informal meetings, consultative (ULC) Formal meetings, authoritative (CSD)
Discursive repertoires	Managerial-structural Fluid-communal
Subjectivities in interaction	Sage on the stage (CSD). Guide on the side (ULC).
Power relations	Central authority controls (CSD) Dispersed power (ULC)
Codes of signification	'Integrity' signifies commitment to the aims set by the district (CSD) 'Integrity' signifies preserving the values and practices of the ULC community (ULC)
Tacit assumptions	Education is about learning valuable knowledge (CSD) Education is about developing the mind (ULC)

participants take up or resist, fully or partially, aspects of its dominant discursive practices.' (p. 181).

Table 6.1 summarises these two different groups in terms of their teaching and learning regimes, though in offering a summary it also characterises them wrongly as two homogeneous, polarised groups.

▶ **Commentary**

This vignette illustrates many of the points made immediately preceding it about the character of the initiative being pursued and the nature of the teaching and learning regimes on the ground. In terms of the initiative itself, alarm bells are rung by its perceived impact on power relations, on subjectivities, and in terms of competing codes of signification for those involved. As far as the TLRs locally are concerned, clearly the huge differences summarised in Table 6.1 had important implications for the possibilities of success. It is worth pursuing this analysis further, following the line of argument taken by Fenwick herself.

Fenwick recognises that workgroups are not based only on discursive consensus: '. . . . within these interactions are myriad microdisconnections and resistances among the logics of different discourses at work' (p. 172). This is true of teaching and learning regimes, where multiple discursive repertoires are found. Different ones can be taken up and then dropped by the same individual. We also see the significance of discursive negotiation, resistance, reconstruction, and compliance.

From this discursive perspective, knowledge and social identities are not fixed but negotiated through different discursive positions and events. But these events are not neutral. Power dynamics infuse all discursive practices, and can both exclude and colonise, as well as amplify and expand. Activities and identities in the educational space are influenced by those discourses and their semiotics (the signs, codes and texts) which are most visible and accorded most authority by different groups sharing that space. These discourses legitimate certain institutions and values and exclude others, by representing 'norms' and casting nonconformists as 'other' to these norms. (pp. 173–174).

One manager's excellence in the discursive strategies of articulation and translation assisted the process of change in that case study. For example, parents of her students claimed she understood their perspective then mirrored it back to them in language capturing the nuances of their meaning and feelings. Meanwhile, teachers claimed that she explained various partners' meanings to one another, adeptly translating concepts into different communities' terms. Other individuals also did discursive work, for example one pupil's father who worked with parents to 'hybridise' the discourse and translate their terms for the school administrators.

Fenwick also acknowledges the problematic nature of intersubjectivity, noting that while there may be apparent shared understanding on the surface, underneath there are different sets of meaning and codes of signification. For example, she notes that terms like 'integrity' and 'core values' were powerful signifiers for both groups, yet what they actually meant and signified was in fact quite different. Similarly, 'research' for ULC was understood in a more 'academic' way while for CSD it meant local, applied studies.

Power issues clearly permeate this story: there are asymmetries of power in the different discourses.

So, for change agents it is important to recognise the frequent lack of intersubjectivity between partners and to dispense with the idea that languages and practices are transparent to the other partners. Being aware of alternative discourses and being prepared to employ them is particularly helpful. The significance of doing discursive work is fundamental in working through the differences among groups. Fenwick talks about 'critical and designing discursive work' which requires myriad language capacities. However, it is more than just a question of discourse. It is also important to have a 'feel for the game' (Bourdieu and Wacquant, 1992): an almost unconscious knowledge of the implicit rules which allow individuals to be successful in a given context. This involves getting to grips with tacit assumptions and conventions of appropriateness which are not always obvious, especially to newcomers.

▶ **Vignette: The significance of congruence between initiative and cultural contexts (adapted from Elton, 2002)**

Elton (2002) shows how the successful dissemination of project work in physics and problem-based learning in medicine was at least partly a result of the compatibility between the teaching and learning approach and the recurrent practices and other moments within those disciplines. Elton says that before the 1960s no UK university engaged in project work. However, by the 1970s all university physics departments had project work on their courses. The roots of this change can be found in the National Council for Technological Awards which introduced a requirement for project work to be included in the courses which it recognised. Physics departments responded most favourably to this and project work spread from that disciplinary base. Elton writes,

> Staff loved project work because it was so close to doing research, and it would be difficult to think of any other reason for the astonishing transfer upwards and outwards in the next few years.
>
> (2002, p. 8)

A similar success story is found in the case of problem-based learning. Starting originally at a Canadian university in the 1960s, it spread to other medical departments over the next 30 years. As in the case of physics, there was a congruence between the innovation and the recurrent practices with which academics were already familiar, although in this case the practices were those of the medical profession rather than its academic incarnation. Problem-based learning began as a way of helping students acquire diagnostic skills. This way of learning is very close to what consultants already do when they make diagnoses: they make links between observation and other cases with which they are familiar.

▶ Commentary

As the quote from Elton at the start of this chapter suggests, the lesson from the examples he chooses is simple: 'choose a topic for dissemination which fits in well with the academic culture of the targeted group'. The theoretical stance set out in this book raises quite a number of questions, and suggests some answers, about how one might identify 'the academic culture' of a group, where one might draw the boundaries of 'the group', how far there can be said to be just one academic culture in any given group, and the extent to which those cultures are likely to be characterised by diversity and conflict as well as consensus and homogeneity. Nonetheless, Elton's general point remains a good one.

The issue, though, is one of knowing to what extent salience, congruence and profitability exist for any particular enhancement initiative in any particular set of contexts, and also understanding where potential sticking points are. For this reason it is important that those proposing and implementing enhancement initiatives should have as much cultural literacy and anthropological awareness as possible. Establishing whether there are sufficient resources and whether the initiative is adequately prioritised is relatively easy. Establishing what the likely reactions will be is entirely another issue, as is predicting the ways in which an initiative will be adapted rather than just adopted.

Planning change

Those behind enhancement initiatives often adopt what seems to be a default position: the rational-purposive approach. Perhaps this is because this is associated with the prevalent managerialist ideology in contemporary higher education. This approach involves target setting, clear definition of goals and rewards of those who achieve them together with sanctions for those who do not. A linear path is planned and progress along it is monitored. Examples are legion in the literature, particularly the organisational development (OD) literature:

> Leadership is necessary to help organisations develop a new vision of what they can be, then [to] mobilise the organisation to change towards the new vision.
>
> (Bennis and Nanus, 1985, pp. 2–3)

Leaders of the organization must have a clear vision of the desired
end state of the entire system [and] a clear commitment to making
significant personal investment in developing and building commitment
[among staff] to an inspirational vision... All of this requires conscious
and explicit planning and managing... It cannot be left to chance or
good intentions.

(Beckhard and Pritchard, 1992, pp. 4 and 15)

By contrast, an ideographic approach to implementing enhancement initiatives leaves space for local interpretation of the details of an initiative
and how it should be put into practice, allowing some degree of shaping of the initiative so that there is better congruence with pre-existing
contexts. Some degree of flexibility is inevitable as projects develop over
time too, so that implementing an initiative in some way 'creates' it: a
project's meaning develops as the project develops. That meaning will
be different in different places, including vertically as well as horizontally,
so that institutional and departmental managers may have quite a different understanding of what a project involves and entails from those
more directly engaging with it and expected to put into practice. Allowing local groups to develop ownership of an initiative through engaging
with it and 'domesticating' it (Wright, 2002) allows it to become theirs. It
is for this reason that 'reinventing the wheel' is not always or necessarily
a bad thing: the newly invented wheel is at least 'our' wheel, and it is
a wheel which we have shaped for the particulars of our context. Low-
resolution initiatives which leave space for local initiative can be more
successful than high-resolution ones in which the specification is highly
detailed:

Reformers who adopt a rational planning mode of educational reform
sometimes expect that they will improve schools if they designed their
policies correctly. They may measure success by fidelity to plan, by
whether predetermined goals are met, and by longevity. Such a tech-
nocratic and top-down approach, however, slights the many ways
in which schools shape reform and teachers employ their 'wisdom
of practice' to produce pedagogical hybrids. Innovations never enter
educational institutions with the previous slate wiped clean.

(Tyack and Cuban, 1995, pp. 82–83)

An ideographic approach also takes the emphasis off central leaders, recognising that their power to change things through rational
planning is rather limited. Indeed to try to impose a central plan on
what is a very diverse and sometimes chaotic environment – part

of what Barnett (2000) has called 'supercomplexity' – is itself not particularly rational:

> A university with many colleges and other program units probably does not have enough centralised intelligence (or information) to impose some standardised strategy on, say, an engineering school, the School of Nursing, and a department of Slavic languages simultaneously.
>
> (Leslie, 1996, p. 105)

So writers on leadership which reject the technical rational approach such as Senge (1990), Rhoades (2000), and Cuthbert (2002) stress the significance of internal networkers who provide dynamism and local leadership are as well as stressing the need for a certain amount of humility on the part of institutional leaders as well as the responsibilities of everyone in the academy for ensuring success.

> The University is not a symphony... It is not playing one piece of music at a time. It does not perform in one building. It does not only (re)interpret scripted scores. And presidents or provosts are not like conductors. They do not start the music – it is already playing when they arrive and continues after they depart. They do not know all the instruments and how they are played. More than that, they should not want to script the pieces even if that were possible. The creativity and dynamism of a university derives from the energy and independence of its players. Universities should promote independent creativity and jamming more than scripting and adherence to central managers' score and interpretations. We need more leaders who: (a) appreciate the music of different units and understand the ongoing changes of and movements within that music, (b) facilitate and support units in getting together, and (c) help persuade musicians to play to existing strengths and to develop new ones.
>
> (Rhoades, 2000, p. 65)

Table 6.2 Rational-purposive and ideographic approaches to change

Rational-purposive	Ideographic
Clear objectives in advance	Goals with space for interpretation ('low-res' initiatives)
Single clear problem to be addressed	Multiple issues wrapped up in a 'single' development, different players, multiple goals

Milestones along the way	Projects develop in the doing of them
Common outcomes expected everywhere	Diverse outcomes in different places
Resource-based levers of change	Cultural awareness and domestication of change
Top-down direction	Diffused responsibilities
Redundancy and 'failure' to be avoided	An initiative may not immediately result in change, but is part of a 'working out' process at local level. Developing a sense of ownership is important
Metaphor – ocean liner. Dominant captain, tightly coupled steering, environment less significant, groups determined by initial plan	Metaphor – yacht in heavy seas. Skilled crew, autonomous decision-making under central direction, environment very significant, responsiveness to conditions

▶ Vignette: The spread of the credit framework in the United Kingdom (adapted from Trowler, 1998)

The credit framework refers to those aspects of the higher education curriculum facilitated by giving credit value to assessed learning. These include modularity, the semester system, franchising of courses, and accreditation of work-based learning and of prior learning. During the 1980s and 1990s a wave of reform swept higher education in the United Kingdom, shifting the curriculum in many institutions in the direction of the credit framework. Woodrow (1993) describes a boom in franchising during the early 1990s as 'a quiet revolution'. Modularisation also saw a boom, particularly in the late 1980s (Fulton and Elwood, 1989), shifting the curriculum away from the linear unitary or joint degree. By the early 1990s about 80% of universities had developed or were committed to developing modular programmes (Robertson, 1994).

Other aspects of the credit framework similarly spread rapidly across the United Kingdom. By 1993 about 65% of universities had all planned to adopt a two-semester structure in place of the traditional three terms (Robertson, 1994). Nearly 85% of universities had introduced or planned to introduce accredited accumulation and transfer scheme while 75% of the pre-1992 universities recognised and accepted credit systems, or at least indicated their willingness to consider credit as a suitable form of intellectual exchange (Robertson, 1994).

Many universities are now reverting to the previous system, but the question is, why was the dissemination of this complex system at that time so rapid? There had been no government directive and there were no direct funding incentives. Studies had been done which found positive advantages for the credit framework, study tours had taken place in the United States, where the framework was already in place, and institutions were encouraged to adopt it by, for example, the Council for National Academic Awards (CNAA, 1990).

The explanation is multi-causal. While there was no direct financial incentive to adopt the framework, more broadly there had been an opening up of higher education and student numbers were expanding (that is until attempts were made to cap numbers by the Conservative government in the early to mid-1990s). Students brought money and so ways were found to cope with larger numbers. To managers the credit framework appeared to offer a good way to deal with the new, mass, higher education (Watson, 1989). Moreover, the system gives centralised control of the curriculum and promised to put more power into the hands of managers who sometimes felt that they had responsibility but no power because of the control that academics wielded. For those academics and managers interested in widening participation and increasing student choice the credit framework also offered perceived advantages. Students could study at their own pace near to their homes and could pick and choose from a selection of subjects on offer. At the same time for those academics and managers interested in effectively preparing students for work, the credit framework offered the chance to move away from traditional curricula to provide new offerings for students who could make selections based upon their preferred career choices. Finally, because there was no central direction determining exactly how the credit framework was implemented within institutions it was a 'low res' initiative, that is one which is not highly specified, has a low resolution, or is 'fuzzy' rather than clearly defined. This allowed different institutions to adapt it to their own needs and make it their own. Sadly this did mean that the ideal of a national system was never realised: each institution developed idiosyncratic versions of what was meant by 'one credit' and had their own systems of accrediting prior learning, for example.

▶ **Commentary**

So part of the reason for the successful dissemination of this innovation so quickly lies in its attractiveness to different ideological persuasions and to its essentially low resolution nature. It offered profitability to a broad church, both academics and managers. In each case the 'profit' was different, but it was there nonetheless. However, credit transfer in practice was very low within the United Kingdom and even lower across Europe: the European Credit Transfer and Accumulation system (ECTS) has been little used.

This is not to say that the ideographic approach in its pure form is always right. There is a danger of Balkanisation if workgroups become competitive and self-serving. Sometimes, difficult individuals need to be dealt with firmly. And there is always a need for strategic direction from above to avoid anarchy and aimlessness. Appropriate decisions need to be taken in any given context about any given initiative about the degree to which there is top-down specification and planning on the one hand, and the allowance of space and local ownership on the other. It is tempting to adopt an 'agribusiness' approach to change, but in many ways a better metaphor in higher education is the 'market garden'. Low resolution plans are more likely to succeed, albeit with different outcomes in different places, than highly rational high resolution ones, with very clear high-stakes outcomes. However, on the other hand, there is always the danger of anarchy and of plans losing their momentum as groups struggle with them without sufficient central direction. Even ownership can have its downside: adapting an innovation locally may not only give ownership, but can mean that the innovation becomes ossified and when its owners move away those who are expected to work with it may not quite understand how it works or what it is. Moreover, its current owners may cosset the innovation, whatever it is, and protect it in the face of better ways of working.

So, there are no easy answers that can be set down in the pages of a book: there is simply no substitute for intelligent planning and careful thought. But the smart planner is the planner with good conceptual tools. Axioms are all very well, but you have to recognise when to apply them (and how to apply them):

Most of the tacit knowledge lies in recognising the situation as one in which the maxim is appropriate – what Klein (1989) calls 'recognition-primed decision making' . . . Making [maxims] explicit may help to draw attention to the context and conditions where it is appropriate to use them; and that is when the 'real' tacit knowledge begins to be disclosed and further learning is more likely to occur.

(Eraut, 2000, p. 124)

Sadly, many planners do not think about implementation strategies much at all. Barnett and Coates (2005), for example, suggest significant changes to the higher education curriculum and the way it is 'delivered'. But, like many other reinvisaging suggestions for higher education, they offer no implementation strategy. Likewise, Middlehurst (1997, p. 138) suggests we 'tear down the walls [of the Academy] and realign...purposes, roles and functions in new ways' but does not explain the implementation strategies for rebuilding. Likewise, Sinnott and Johnson (1996) set out a

> radically new vision of how the university might become a special sort of workplace/community of thinkers and doers, working together to understand and solve real human problems, in a competitive global market.

But they do not offer much in the way of advice or detail on how this might be achieved.

It is very important to avoid deficit models both in discourse and in the new practices and tools that are proposed. Better to find good practice on the ground and work to develop that than to attempt to introduce something which essentially says to street level bureaucrats (Lipsky, 1980): you need to forgo your old practices completely and work with something shinier and better.

It is important, too, to think clearly about the theories which underpin any proposed new tools and practices and the ways in which they are expected to be implemented and worked with. Too often policy-makers and street level bureaucrats operate on the basis of patchy, poor, and tacit theories. Making theories explicit and subjecting them to robust testing will enhance the chances of success.

It is possible to work to create a receptive climate for new tools and new practices: thinking about rewards as well as appropriate sanctions, and about discourses and the other elements of particular teaching and learning regimes which may be receptive to change will help create a climate in which change is more likely.

► How to fail?

The converse of the above advice – in other words, advice to those who wish to fail – would be as follows:

First, look for single, high-fidelity, right answers. That is, develop pre-defined and clearly outlined solutions to problems that are specified by you: a 'vision'. Visions can exclude others, particularly those on the ground who have different perceptions of the 'the problem' and different notions of what the solutions might be. Sometimes those on the ground do not think there is a 'problem' at all, or think that the 'problem' has different causes (for example, it is the poor quality of the students, rather than our outdated practices). Where this kind of marked difference in perceptions is the case, an excellent way to fail is to go about imposing pre-defined solutions to a problem that is not even recognised as such.

Second, see proposed changes in practices or tools in isolation from the changing context of higher education and the multiple pressures on academics in the current context. A really good way to fail is to get very enthusiastic about a single project: the teaching–research nexus, a new information technology learning tool, problem-based learning, student portfolios, or whatever. Perhaps funding has been made available, so that one or two people are concentrating on this one issue. In such a case it is very easy to forget the multiple pressures, multiple agendas, and the time constraints of those on the ground. It is also easy to forget that not everyone is quite so enthusiastic, and that there are usually new problems associated with every 'solution'. Being unrealistic and somewhat blinkered is a great way to fail.

Third, see any innovations in practices or in tools in isolation from lecturers' subjectivities, their different ideologies, and their recurrent practices as they exist at the moment. Any change will be fitted into a context which already exists, and that context will have a significant effect on the way the change is perceived and implemented. Adoption, adaptation, rejection, or fundamental reconstruction may occur. So a good way to fail is to expect that an innovation will just be 'taken up' regardless of context because it is valuable in its own right.

Fourth, forget the importance of the perception that it 'was invented here': in other words, forget about the significance of local ownership and domestication. Academics are professionals and they rarely happily engage in practices which are imposed or which they have not adapted to their own particular students, discipline, and institutional context. Offering a 'shrink-wrapped' innovation and expecting it to be used straight out of the box is unrealistic.

Fifth, think only about individuals and about changing organisations through individual change and try to forget about groups and group processes as well as organisational structures and systems when planning change of any significance. Changes based on 'improving' the individual will usually be a disappointment if not done with an awareness of the context individuals operate in and how they see the situation. It is easy to blame individuals, groups, or departments as being 'difficult': complacent, resistant to change, and stuck in outdated but comfortable ways.

The word 'dinosaur' is often used here for its many connotations. But this thinking is both reductionist and based on a deficit model, which is never a good place from which to initiate change. Such thinking inhibits an exploration of the reasons for such attitudes and a perspective which acknowledges that there are multiple versions of what the problem is (if any) and what should be done about it (if anything). A view which adopts a more analytical and structural perspective is more likely to result in an implementation plan that will work. Peter Knight and I have written more about this in Knight and Trowler, 2001, especially Chapters 1 and 3.

Sixth, forget about the backstory: about narratives that participants have about their history and their context. Think about new practices and tools being introduced in a static and ahistorical environment only and forget about process. So, in order to fail, it is best to think about individuals without a departmental, disciplinary, and institutional context, and ones who have no history in those things, or stories about that.

Seventh, expect there to be consensus on the ground about an innovation. Imagine that there are shared attitudes, values, and agendas. Do not think for a moment that there will be conflict, emotional turmoil, and power plays. And most of all do not take such eventualities into account in any planning you do around the implementation of the innovation (though, of course, to guarantee failure there should never be an implementation plan at all – simply a wonderful vision).

And of course very significantly linked to failure are the factors which Cerych and Sabatier told us about in 1986: under-fund the project, give it leadership which is sometimes strong and sometimes absent, keep changing the focus so that goals are unclear; offer multiple new tools and practices together, especially in a bundle which contains inherent mutual contradictions; and do all this in an environment which itself is rich in innovations and pressures, and is generally as turbulent as possible.

► What should we expect when we try to enhance teaching and learning?

A good theoretical understanding of change should refine our radar, help us to make at least fuzzy predictions about change processes. It should help us to foresee and avoid likely pitfalls, to understand what might work and what probably won't, and to get a feel for how far we should expect our desired outcomes to come to fruition and how far compromises must be made and expectations limited.

Though we like to imagine that *everyone* will win from changes that we put in place, almost *every* enhancement initiative will have differential costs and benefits. There will be losers and winners in terms of identities, power relations, and emotional responses.

From the point of view of those on the ground – Lipsky's street level bureaucrats – it is important to be constantly mindful that fundamental change usually involves struggle between competing ideologies and interests. It is often difficult to distinguish between change initiatives which really are in the interests of the greater good and those which serve the minority. For example, the pressure to ensure and enhance quality, to empower students, and to increase social mobility and equity might at the same time disempower and perhaps even proletarianise professionals, impoverishing their work and in the end leaving students without a range of experiences and qualities that higher education has traditionally sought to imbue. Taking the case of pressure from quality assurance bodies to provide students with statements of learning outcomes, Nixon *et al.* (2001, p. 231) warn us to beware attempts to 'coral academic professionalism within the parameters of outcome statements and competence thresholds'. The discourses of performativity today appear to be everywhere and, from some perspectives at least, they operate in the interests of the powerful few.

When emotional satisfaction is denied through preventing people from achieving their own goals, being compelled to realise other people's goals, then there will be rejection.

> The feeling of freedom and improvisation in planning was exceptionally important to our sample teachers. It offered the opportunity to let the ideas and the brainstorming with colleagues flow.... Our data suggest that rational planning models are...flawed because they take no account of emotion. Among the work that teachers do, and among those who try to shape that work, even planning should be approached as an emotional practice.
>
> (Hargreaves, 1998, pp. 849–850)

There will almost always be refraction and domestication of the change initiative. Workgroups and the individuals within them will often use coping strategies, policy reconstruction, or simple avoidance as well as compliance (including ritualistic compliance) in ways which subvert, change, or simply block policy initiatives.

Tools will be used in unexpected ways. Workgroups will take up and use new tools in ways which both affect and are affected by the workgroups' practices: these tools will be used in different ways in different places and, again, the consequences of this differential use are unpredictable.

Chapter 1 suggested that it is most productive to view universities as protean phenomena with multiple cultures that are dynamic in character so that their parts respond differently to change initiatives. Universities, as Alvesson (2002) tells us, have multiple cultural configurations. There are many departments and even workgroups within departments, each of which is on a day-to-day basis generating practices that will become recurrent and ways of seeing the world as well as enacting those which are already in existence. In doing so they are creating a system of cultural diversity within a single institution. This means that change initiatives will be received differently in different places even within small universities. How they are received, interpreted, and subsequently implemented will lead to different outcomes in different parts of universities. The case studies throughout this book illustrate this.

Again, the health warning to not forget structure should be restated: workgroups are not completely agentic. Structure and agency together are in mutual operation and structures limit and condition what can be done and what outcomes are. But workgroups do have sufficient discretion and power in terms of the social construction of reality to influence the reception and implementation of change in very significant ways and so outcomes will be different in different places. Studies of change initiatives – for example, of marketisation in the British compulsory education system (Bowe *et al.*, 1992) – have demonstrated this.

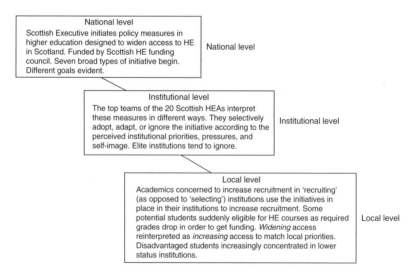

Figure 6.1 The implementation staircase: A simplified example (adapted from Morgan-Klein and Murphy, 2002)

Workgroups do not only operate in horizontal relationship to each other in a nested way. In addition, initiatives are dealt with in a vertical way, moving up and down an implementation staircase (Figure 6.1) (Reynolds and Saunders, 1987). As they move, initiatives are refracted at each level and so what moves up, and down, the staircase is significantly different. So, it is important to think vertically, about interdependencies at higher and lower levels of analysis, as well as horizontally, about sequential interrelatedness. Unless there is flow back up the implementation staircase (feedback, or 'backward mapping' as Dyer, 1999, calls it), poor practices can continue and mistakes will be repeated with no learning loop occurring.

People on the ground and planners will develop their own, different, perspectives on the situations. Elsewhere (Trowler and Knight, 2001) I have shown that we can expect that planners, and even practitioners-as-planners, will lose sight of local diversity and constraints, of the 'rough terrain' that always exists in the messiness on the ground. This is because they operate as *planners* in a workgroup whose task is planning, not practice. There will be contextual simplification – planners will tend to forget about the diversity of issues and the complexity of practice that face street level bureaucrats. There will be causal simplification: planners will tend to see a simple, linear cause-and-effect path and forget about the multiple factors which impinge on and condition practice on the ground, throwing off practices from those desired by planners. There will be contextual occlusion: parts of practice will be 'clouded' and obscured, forgotten about in significant and to some extent predictable ways. And finally there will be obliteration of meaning and affect as planners forget that, for those on the ground, practices and meaning mutually instantiate each other: the emotional life of the street level bureaucrats is bound up in what they do and why they do it as well as how they understand it. Professional life is not just about the cognitive, it also engages the heart. Meanwhile, for people on the ground enhancement initiatives, coming together with lots of other innovations in their professional lives, may feel like just another passing fad, or another issue to be dealt with in busy professional lives. Innovation fatigue sets in quickly but has long-lasting effects. It is also very common:

More than half of those [innovators] who responded to a question about attitudes commented that their colleagues considered the innovation to be unnecessary, too time-consuming or threatening.

(Hannan and Silver, 2000, p. 8)

What Earley *et al.* (2002) say of leaders in schools applies equally well to academics:

> Leaders in schools are de-motivated by over-bearing bureaucracy and excessive paperwork and also by 'constant change' in the education system. Balancing work and home life is an increasing concern and more work is needed to make school leadership both an attractive and do-able task.

We know, too, that change is slow. Existing cultures are extremely tenacious: cultural sensitivity is very important in devising change strategies, but even then expect intertia. Joe Farrell's study of change (2000) in the United States tells us just how slow things can be and just how tenacious existing cultures are. So, much more often than phase changes, transformation, or reinvention, we see small-scale, incremental, bricolage changes. Existing practices largely remain in place with a few changes here and there subtly modifying them and the meanings associated with them over time.

▶ Conclusion

From a sociocultural perspective, then, any understanding of change processes needs to adopt a perspective rather wider than that normally used by change theorists in, for example, the organisational development tradition (see p. 8). In particular, it needs to develop a clear perspective on the sets of social practices on the ground, and their associated moments. Any attempt to introduce change, for example, a new teaching technique or a new priority, will involve throwing a new element into the complex mix of social practices, their moments, and the dynamic networks in which they reside.

If there are no natural boundaries and there is interconnectedness then there is no natural or obvious place at which to pitch the level or focus of analysis. The level of analysis chosen for intervention affects in crucial ways the salient features: that is to say, scale issues come into operation. Teaching and learning enhancement policies rarely consider the most appropriate points and levels at which interventions should be aimed: should they be at the level of the individual, the department, the institution, the discipline, or where? Too often there are multiple agencies and individuals attempting, without coordination, to improve learning and teaching. This is sometimes called the 'Christmas tree' model of policy development: plenty of pretty lights and shiny baubles, but they do not last long, have little relationship to each other and do not have any lasting effect on normal daily life (Trowler and Bamber, 2005).

A focus on change in higher education at the macro level brings to prominence socio-economic structures, government policies, and broader social conditions as well as (at a slightly lower level) institutional cultures and structures. A focus at the meso level brings to salience micro-social processes at the small group level, while that at the micro level brings issues of subjectivities and interpretive matrices to prominence. Putting one aspect of social reality into sharp relief blurs others, though there are intimate and important connections between them.

7 Researching for Change

► **Why research for change?**

This chapter considers some of the issues involved in researching for change aimed at enhancement. Some readers may consider this section of the book not relevant to their needs. However, Bensimon *et al.* (2004, p. 105) suggest that it is important for practitioners concerned with change to 'produce knowledge in local contexts to identify problems and take action to solve them'. These authors advocate the idea that change agents should be 'practitioners-as-researchers'. While change is not always about solving problems, action research of the sort they recommend is very significant if change efforts are to be informed by evidence rather than ignorance or fuzzy perceptions. Action research involves a circle of data gathering, analysis, action based on the evidence collected, and then further data gathering. Enquiry-based evidence helps underpin the careful thinking that is necessary if enhancement efforts are to succeed. In addition, I have argued in earlier chapters that successful change involves careful analysis of innovations, context, and the interactions between them. Congruence and salience are key issues, for example, and coming to an understanding of the character of changes as they impact, or are likely to impact, on the ground requires information gathering of one form or another.

Thinking about change also needs to be well informed conceptually and theoretically. Boyce (2003) points out that fundamental organisational learning which addresses core values and practices (the so-called 'double loop learning') and which brings about long-lasting organisational change requires 'rigorous organizational inquiry: continuous practice of examining assumptions, surfacing and challenging mental models, and acting on what is learned' (p. 128). This development of new mental models is very significant. In the context of this book these models relate to the ways an organisation and any innovation introduced into it are perceived and understood. Developing useful mental models requires both sound information *and* illuminative concepts and theories. The earlier parts of this book have attempted to offer the latter.

Thinking and researching for change needs to address three things: the characteristics of any proposed innovation; those of the context of its introduction; and finally, the relationship between innovation and

158

context. Earlier chapters have shown how efforts to enhance teaching, learning, assessment, and curriculum are likely to be filtered through teaching and learning regimes in very significant ways. The salience of initiatives to workgroups, the degree of congruence that initiatives have with existing practices and attitudes, and the profitability (at least potentially) for members of workgroups all have very significant consequences for the 'success' of enhancement initiatives. We have seen, too, how it is likely that change efforts will become 'domesticated' in different contexts, leading to different outcomes in different places. Research into practice, then, affords the opportunity to study not only teaching and learning regimes themselves but also the nature of change initiatives, the relationship between those initiatives and cultures on the ground, as well as the trajectories that initiatives follow as they move through the path of implementation.

In addition to its value to the practitioner-as-researcher, the study of teaching and learning regimes affords the opportunity of studying and exposing the roles of power, emotion, and subjectivities in practices associated with teaching, learning, and assessment in higher education. These areas are often missing in the study of learning and teaching. So, in terms of value to the practitioner interested in change and in terms of the focus on previously under-researched substantive areas, researching teaching and learning regimes in change contexts represents very interesting and fertile ground.

▶ Health warnings

In conducting studies in this area, it is particularly important to make clear analytical choices about the boundaries of research: what is included and what is excluded in the research questions. It is very easy in this kind of research to stray into interesting areas that are connected with the main focus but to be quickly deluged with data and issues that make analysis and write-up very difficult. This is especially prevalent in team projects and projects, as is likely here, where there is an institutional interest in the results. In these cases each team member brings a particular set of interests to the table and institutional representatives may want to focus on particular areas that *they* consider the most significant issues for their university. The project quickly accretes new areas and new objectives in an enthusiastic discussion about what might be achieved. But a sense of realism is lost, only to be regained in the cold light of data aggregation and analysis. The key question is, if this is research for change, what are the reasons for collecting data, and what kinds of data will best inform the change process?

Related to this is an issue which can be summed up in the question 'whose problem?' Dale (1989) and Ozga (2000) distinguish between three research 'projects'. The social administration project is reformist, attempting to improve the lot of the clients: in our case, students. Research in the social administration tradition in higher education is aimed at improving the student experience and making student learning more effective and efficient. A second research approach is the policy analysis project. Here policy-making is taken as the preserve of government and managers, the role of the researcher is not to question the policy but to ensure that social policies are delivered regardless of content, who the beneficiaries are, or what priorities have been selected. The third approach is the 'social science project'. Here the 'problem' is not the client's and neither is it the policy-maker's. Rather it is to some extent defined in terms of theory and the literature in the area. Its concerns involve a mix of attempting to gain a better understanding of how things work, contributing to theory and perhaps 'making' rather than 'taking' problems in the area of investigation – in other words, to propose new issues and concerns that neither policy-makers nor clients have identified. While both the social administration and the policy analysis projects are, in different ways, technicist, the social science project is more conceptual in character.

In just the same way, action research in general can be undertaken with different audiences, beneficiaries, and purposes in mind. Action research can be emancipatory in intent, aiming to identify disadvantaged groups and to rectify structural disadvantage, or it can simply be aimed at making sure policy is implemented effectively, regardless of what it is or its effects.

The point is not to say that one is better than other, rather to make the comment that researchers should be clear that they are (whether they know it or not) making choices about the project they are engaged in. It is better to make this choice in a knowledgeable way, with an awareness of roads not followed and their advantages, rather than blindly.

At a more technical level, in any research project it is also important to establish alignment between the research questions (which need to be clearly specified, answerable, and of significance to a wide audience) on the one hand and the research design on the other. The research design needs to be such that the following questions can be answered in the affirmative: 'will this research design give me the right kind of data to answer these questions?' and 'will the research design provide convincing answers to these questions?'.

Choices need to be made on clearly articulated grounds. Important choices include those about methods of data collection, the nature of the sample selected for the study, the focus of study, methods of analysis, and the extent to which implications for practice can and should be inferred from research findings. The extent to which truth claims can be justifiably made also needs careful thought.

Finally, it is important to reiterate that the practitioner-as-researcher does not confuse ontological substance with analytical abstractions. Teaching and learning regimes are an analytical abstraction, developed to assist in conceptualising social processes and to theorise about linkages within the social world. As noted earlier, confusing one's model of reality with the reality of the model (Bourdieu, 1977, p. 29) can lead to claims about the nature of reality which cannot be substantiated.

▶ Researching for change: Special issues

It is fairly obvious that ethnographic research is particularly suited to any study interested in gaining depth knowledge of practices, attitudes, and values at local level. Ethnography is the fine-grained study of particular cultures normally through the use of multiple methods, the aim being to develop at least a 'thick description' (Geertz, 1983) of the cultural contexts. These methods usually include in-depth semi-structured interviews; observation (sometimes participant observation); diary-keeping, and the careful study of relevant documentation. Many of the textbooks on methodology include accounts of ethnographic procedures and I do not intend to reproduce those here. The problem with ethnography is that it is very labour-intensive if done properly. For practitioners-as-researchers this is a major drawback. The key concern is to gather data quickly and to apply it to policy development and implementation. Moreover, ethnography directs the analytical gaze towards *culture* and not, for example, on other areas of interest such as the characteristics of change initiatives or policy trajectories. In addition to these problems, ethnographic methods may not be particularly good at addressing some of the unique challenges researching workgroups and change pose. I address these next.

1. *The 'beyond methodological individualism' problem.* The socio-cultural approach discussed here takes as its unit of analysis the workgroup. Many of the standard approaches to research in the social sciences are based on methodological individualism (MI). This is an approach to social research which assumes that the thoughts and decisions of individual people have very significant effects because social institutions like universities are little more than collective products of the decisions and actions of individuals. The easy solution to data collection is usually something like semi-structured interviews with individual academics. The question is, however, do a series of individual 'takes' provide a composite picture

of the social group? The answer is probably 'no'. From a sociocultural perspective the whole is greater than the sum of its parts.

2. *The problem of capturing the impalpable.* Much of the discussion in the earlier part of the book refers to implicit or emotional dimensions of knowing and meaning. Indeed some implicit knowledge may be impossible to describe in a meaningful way (how to deliver a lecture in a way which is both intellectually rigorous and engaging, for example). Even apparently 'simple' explicit knowledge is often combined with tacit knowing. Eraut (2000) distinguishes between codified knowledge ready for use; knowledge acquired through acculturation; knowledge constructed from experience, social interaction, and reflection; skills; episodes, impressions, and images; and feelings. He points out that in professional areas these are nearly always combined. Jarvis (1999) also shows how content knowledge, tacit knowledge, process knowledge, and beliefs and values form a mix in practitioners' knowledge. Tacit knowing and feelings are very hard to capture through normal data collection methods. In the discipline called knowledge management the process of 'knowledge harvesting' involves interviewing experts with a view to capturing and then codifying the nature of their knowledge. However, this works well only with relatively simple forms of knowing and in areas which are quite clearly delimited.

3. *The problem of knowledge accumulation.* One of the key tenets of sociocultural theory is the notion of situational contingency: that the characteristics of particular contexts are very significant in conditioning what works there (and what does not), what is considered 'true' knowledge, and what is seen as 'just common sense'. These ideas (sometimes referred to as situated cognition and situated rationality) mean that any findings of research are similarly limited to the contexts in which the research was done. Such limited truth claims can mean that research into local cultures has limited value unless a good response to this problem can be found. That response is usually different from study to study. Where case study research is presented it is important that the purposes of the study are clear to the writer and that they work to make the study easy for readers to connect to, be it analytically, experientially, practically, or personally (Stevenson, 2004). The reader too has a responsibility: they need to approach case studies with clear issues and questions in mind concerning what the case can offer and the extent to which it can be adopted and used (Ottewill *et al.*, 2002). The practitioner-as-researcher can help prepare them for this.

4. *The problem of occluded structures.* Any research conducted at the micro or meso level is in danger of being blind to the effects of macro

influences; of structures which condition and constrain behaviour. When the individual or social group is taken as the unit of analysis it may be the case that they themselves cannot see the ways in which the discourse, practices, and ideas are conditioned by wider forces. This is not an inevitable feature of fine-grained research, particularly where the researcher is aware of the issue. It remains, however, a constant danger. This is particularly so where the researcher and the researched are members of the same cultural group.

5. *The 'simplicity versus nuance' dilemma.* Achieving a balance between ideographic and nomothetic approaches is always an issue. I noted earlier that ideographic approaches to research are those which do not attempt to impose external categories or understandings on a culture, but rather to represent that culture from an insider's perspective. By contrast, nomothetic approaches attempt to generalise across cultures, develop law-like statements, and move from the particular characteristics of a community to broader analytical categories. Rogoff (2003) argues that nomothetic (or what he calls 'imposed') approaches are usually inappropriate and insufficiently congruent with the situation of the community being studied.

Smith agrees, contrasting these 'imposed' with 'derived' research approaches:

> social scientists who impose their categories on the lives of people they study without regard for the lived experiences of these very people ... are articulating elements of the past with new ones in quite different ways and these will be read in very different ways by specific audiences at different times and places. [They take] little account of the complex conditions in which meanings are produced and, as a result, miss ... the ways in which meanings and cultural boundaries are constantly moving.
>
> (Smith, 2000, p. 15)

By contrast, in the derived approach, the researcher 'adapts ways of questioning, serving and interpreting to fit the perspective of the participants' (p. 31). While being desirable, this raises special problems about the transferability of research findings from context to context, and hence about the cumulative nature of the knowledge derived. This is especially true, for example, in researching codes of signification which are almost inevitably context-bound, as we saw in Chapter 4. For the practitioner-as-researcher any parochial, anecdotal flavour raises the danger that readers (perhaps senior managers or policy-makers) will discount their findings. So, this dilemma is one which concerns the potential of doing considerable damage to the nuanced, protean, and situated nature of cultural manifestations on the one hand and being of limited research value on the other.

A balance needs to be sought, then, between the heuristically valuable nomothetic approach and the more nuanced but situationally specific ideographic one. Hart and Conn (1990) argue that case studies are a valuable way of studying the interactions between situational characteristics and actions. In particular, they recommend longitudinal case studies which identify critical issues and periods of transition followed by more detailed case studies. They believe that general principles of behaviour can be generated by fully understanding a case study, so that 'cumulation' of knowledge can occur despite the apparently unique character of the situation under study. Moreover, they argue that case studies can be combined with other research methods, including aggregated data. A multi-study, multi-method approach like this is also advocated by Hormuth (1990). This, he argues, 'has provided the chance to identify general patterns of results and separate them from isolated findings that make little sense in the context of...complete research programme[s]' (p. 201). However, the practitioner-as-researcher who is primarily interested in getting change right may not be able to adopt such a sophisticated research design.

6. *The problem of historicity.* Sociocultural theory in general and the concept of teaching and learning regimes in particular includes an understanding of social life as dynamic and rooted in history. The concept of the 'backstory' is very significant: narratives about the history of the social group are very important to its self-image and condition how it behaves in the present. Getting access to the backstory, and the potentially diverse narratives about it, raises an additional issue for anyone interested in researching local cultures with a view to enhancing practices.

7. *The sensitivities problem.* Any fine-grained research raises questions of getting access to research sites and dealing with sensitive issues as well as the standard ethical ones. Exploring the distribution of power, enquiring into individual subjectivities and interactions between them, and trying to understand the emotional dynamics of particular situations raise potentially intractable problems for the researcher, particularly when HEIs have become very protective of their 'brand'. Of course there are some simple measures that can be put in place: being careful to go through any ethical procedures required; giving respondents a full outline of the nature of the research; being absolutely clear about rigorous procedures to ensure anonymity; offering respondents

the right to amend or even place a veto on the publication of parts of the research derived from data emanating from them. Such measures can help put respondents at their ease, but skill and sensitivity on the part of the researcher is also required. Here the practitioner-as-researcher may have advantages: the research may not be for publication and gaining institutional permission might not be a problem if there is clear potential benefit. There are disadvantages to this insider role too, however.

8. *The insider–outsider problem.* Finally, there are advantages to conducting research within one's own organisation. This 'insider' research means that the researcher is culturally literate and so able to interpret phenomena in the ways that members of the social group being researched do, at least to some extent. They also have access to the 'second record' (Hull, 1985; Stenhouse, 1979): the underlying meanings or unintended significance of statements made. They are in short able to 'read between the lines'. However, being an insider means there is potential confusion between one's research role and one's professional role which may potentially 'pollute' the data. Like other insiders, the researcher may also find it difficult to identify structural influences (see point 4 above). Their impartiality may also be in doubt, and indeed for novice researchers it is often hard to put aside one's professional commitments. Outsider researchers lose the advantages of insider research but do not suffer from its disadvantages: what they lose in insight they gain in distance. Neither approach is perfect.

These are research issues which are fairly specific to the issues raised in this book. There are also some enduring questions which much social science research has to address. Foremost amongst these is the question of the relationship between attitudes, beliefs, and assumptions on the one hand and practices on the other. Kane *et al.* (2002, p. 196) make the point that for researchers concerned with enhancing teaching and learning practices in universities 'it is imperative that we understand how the links between beliefs and practices are made'. Their review of literature in this area shows that research design often takes no account of the differences between 'espoused theories' (as articulated in interviews) and 'theories-in-use' (as applied during episodes of professional practice). Yet studies like Fanghanel's (2004) which have unpicked the dissonances between beliefs, statements, and practices as well as the (non-)transfer of learned practices from one context to another have demonstrated the multiple reasons why such dissonances exist. It is not surprising then that they are very common. Nonetheless, much of the research in the area makes no attempt to distinguish between beliefs and practices or to theorise the links between the two, for example, assuming that what academics say they believe and do is what they actually do. Clearly, there is often dissonance between values and practice, as Becher and Kogan (1992) demonstrate. Appropriate research design combined with truth claims which are carefully limited to what can actually be sustained from the data are two obvious ways in which some of these problems can be avoided.

► Some potential solutions at the individual level

The standard approaches to research could be used to study teaching and learning regimes, and I will not deal with those much-explored methods here. In considering the potential solutions to some of the above knotty issues that go beyond these standard approaches one possibility is to use *hybridised methodologies*, that is to combine two or more data-gathering approaches.

Thus, for example, one could use card-sorting techniques together with discourse analysis (semantic) or quantitative analysis (syntactic) methods. In card-sorting, a set of statements related to the topic of interest are generated, perhaps a hundred or so. The statements may be derived from the literature, from brainstorming, from focus groups, or from interviews conducted prior to using this method. Then a set of cards is produced on which is written one statement and its opposite. Respondents are asked to sort the cards into three piles: a pile in which the upper statement is true; a pile in which the lower statement (its opposite) is true; and the rest.

If a quantitative or syntactic approach is taken the respondents may then be asked to sort the first two piles into Likert-like order (very true, quite true, true, only just true). In this case, cluster analysis or multidimensional scaling can be used. Software such as *EZsort* and *Websort* is also available for this kind of analysis. The journal *Expert Systems* (2005, pp. 3, 22) discusses this kind of approach.

► Card-sorting – Some examples of statements

- I think/don't think the department puts an emphasis on teaching as part of our duties.
- Every module has/doesn't have a module leader who makes the ultimate choices.
- In my department we talk/don't talk freely about what we do in the classroom.

- Some departments have eccentric mavericks who cause trouble. We do/don't.
- I guess we pretty much agree/disagree on what we are doing in the courses we provide.
- The department itself is fairly open/closed in terms of teaching strategies.
- My department is/isn't very committed to the question of 'diversity'.
- Practices and attitudes about teaching and learning in the department are/aren't mainly laid down by the academic leader

Longer statements can also be used, for example, quotes from interviews conducted prior to the card-sorting exercise:

There is a departmental approach, yes. All core lectures have to be on Blackboard, and then every year we analyse the marks and you have external examiners who check that as well and any time your average – say if I have a higher average or a lower average – I have to write an explanation of it and if my marks are not spread properly.

In more qualitative (semantic) approaches to card-sorting the respondents may be interviewed about the reasons for their choices in sorting the cards into each of the three piles, and in this case, techniques such as discourse analysis might be applied to give an insight into the social situations which they refer to.

A further elaboration of this idea is to use projective techniques after a card-sorting exercise. Projective techniques involve asking respondents to imagine themselves in the shoes of another person, or to imagine alternative situations in which they might project their responses. Such techniques are another way of accessing taken-for-granted knowledge. In this instance, the respondent, in discussing the rationale for their own choices of card selection, could be asked to project themselves into the minds of relevant others and to compare their hypothesised responses with those actually made by the respondent. This is particularly useful for uncovering tensions, conflicts, and alternative positions within a teaching and learning regime.

Another example of hybridised methods is the use of insider research together with an outsider discussant. Insider research has both advantages and disadvantages: while the researcher is culturally literate, they may also share with the respondents certain ways of seeing the world which limit the researcher's perspective. Most practitioners-as-researchers will be insiders of course, at least to some extent. Introducing an outsider to observe the situation and to respond to the insider's perceptions of it helps to mitigate some of the disadvantages of insider research, offering a different perspective on the social situation.

Another example of hybrid method is image-based data gathering plus in-depth interviewing. Drawings of the way things might be working are produced by the researcher (as happens in Soft Systems Methodology, for example, Checkland and Scholes, 1999) for comment by respondents. Photographs might be used in a similar way to elicit a reaction. Alternatively, respondents may be asked to create sociograms, to depict their own social situation graphically, or to comment on such drawings produced by others in their social situation. The subsequent in-depth interview allows the researcher to come at the meanings and understandings captured in images or the interpretation of them in an indirect way, and to access those meanings which might be only tacit for the respondents.

Projective techniques, as noted above, can be very useful in uncovering differences in perspective, competing positions, and areas of tension within a TLR. As well as combining them with card-sorting exercises, other possible combinations include personal narratives (for example, asking the respondent to relate their own role in a critical incident that occurred in the context of interest – see, for example, Entwistle and Walker, 2002) or the use of the vignettes as a catalyst for discussing the respondent's reaction (see, for example, the vignette about the 'New Route doctoral programme' on pp. 78–80). In both these cases the respondent could be asked to project the reactions of significant others from their professional context.

Finally, the practitioner-as-researcher may choose to use oblique questions together with discourse analysis techniques. Oblique questions come at the issue of interest in an indirect way, and the analysis is also inferential rather than direct. Thus, for example, one might ask the respondent to describe the most professional academic they have ever met, or to answer the question 'was there ever a golden age in higher education?' The responses to such questions can provide insights into the respondent's notion of professionalism or their idea of what constitutes preferred practices and situations. Combining this with discourse analysis of the whole text produced by the respondent can offer even greater depth to the analysis.

▶ Some potential solutions at the group level

The suggestions above are all based on data collection with individuals, and I have already alluded to some of the problems associated with MI. Given that workgroups are the primary unit of analysis in the study of teaching and learning regimes it makes sense that research should involve groups too. This also has its problems of course: the dominant individual; the way the group dynamics shaped the discussion; the inhibiting nature of talking in groups; the tendency of groups to try to balance opinions, or sometimes get carried away with one side of an argument. These as well as several other issues become apparent when collecting data in group contexts.

However, a well thought-through approach to data collection can serve to mitigate some of these problems and instead to highlight the advantages of collecting data in groups. These include the real-time discussion of alternative points of view, tensions, and conflicts; the illumination of shared understandings and discourse; the ways in which subjectivities and the exercise of power differences occur even in simply researching group dynamics.

One way of structuring data collection from a group of colleagues is to ask them to discuss real-life episodes that they have shared. Retrospective discussion can be extremely revealing, particularly when they focus on where the problems were, how things moved on, who were the key individuals, and what were the key events. The researcher's role as 'chair' is absolutely crucial here to ensure that the data are relevant to the research questions and are as rich as possible.

An alternative and slightly safer approach is for the researcher to describe incidents or tell stories about events that have not actually happened to the respondents. Case studies or stories about problematic issues can be particularly useful. Such an approach means that sensitivities are less likely to be touched and has the advantage that the researcher can develop vignettes which are likely to result in data which are rich with respect to the research questions. A further alternative is to use mediating artefacts such as pictures, case notes, or documents as catalysts for discussion. In this case it is often better to provide such artefacts to participants in advance so that they have time to reflect on them.

Another approach, often used in *knowledge harvesting*, is to ask participants to demonstrate practices and skills with a commentary, and in a group context the other participants are able to do likewise and to comment on each other's performance. Of course, one particular issue here is the potential difficulty of getting agreement from participants to spend time and effort doing this sort of activity. The ability to demonstrate some form of profitability for them is very useful in this – for example stressing the developmental aspects of such a group activity in terms of making enhancement efforts as appropriate and effective as possible.

Finally, it may be possible to encourage respondents to apply concepts and theories to make sense of their experience, or at least to enquire about the extent to which theory can be usefully applied. This involves introducing respondents to relevant concepts and theory in a careful and appropriate way and then questioning them about their response to their applicability. This of course can be done in an individual as well as a group context of data collection, and is in fact an approach derived from the individualistic 'personal construct theory'.

► Making the normal strange

As already mentioned, one of the problems practitioners-as-researchers in general are faced with is the fact that aspects of familiar cultures tend to be invisible: taken for granted, unreflectively accepted. This is true both for the person doing the research and for their respondents. As Garfinkel (1967, p. 37) says, for ' . . . background expectancies to come into view one must either be a stranger to the "life as usual" character of everyday scenes, or become estranged from them'. Therefore many of the usual methods of data collection such as questionnaires or interviews are unlikely to yield much interesting data about cultural characteristics.

There are a number of ways around this problem.

First, the enquiry can privilege newcomers to the cultural scene in its research design. The fresh eyes of a cultural neophyte can offer valuable insights into contextual characteristics. They are able to see things which are not visible to the old hands. Often they will express surprise, even shock ('culture shock'), at some of the recurrent practices, values, and attitudes and unconsidered assumptions that they find.

Second, the practitioner-as-researcher can look for contentious issues which expose cultural characteristics. If one uses the metaphor of culture as a river with tributaries and a clear direction and strength of flow, then these issues are rocks in the stream. They create turbulence. They cause the current to effervesce, exposing the stream to observation. They interrupt the flow for a moment. Thus the whether-and-how of accrediting prior experiential learning can expose assumptions about knowledge appropriate in the academy. Implicit theories of teaching can be tested by bringing up approaches to teaching and learning that may challenge assumptions or conventions of appropriateness.

A third approach is to move outside the workgroup of interest altogether and gather data from other sources who are familiar with the workgroup but not strictly part of it. Like the newcomer, such respondents have fresh eyes. Examples might be the administrators in a department who are not themselves involved in teaching and learning but who are party to a variety of kinds of information about practices in the department. Moving further outside the workgroup, those in university learning development centres over the years gather a considerable amount of information from their 'clients'about departmental practices and the differences across the university in terms of teaching, learning, and assessment. Finally, students themselves who are studying across two or more departments (for example, those on combined degree schemes) gain valuable insights because of the variety of their experience. The same is true of ex-students who, from the vantage point of their new context, are able to look with fresh eyes at their learning experience and the practices and attitudes that contributed to it.

▶ Researching the initiative

The bulk of the chapter so far has been concerned with researching context. This is because the most challenging issues are raised here. There remains, however, the question of researching the initiative itself and the relationship between the initiative and the context. In a sense these are simpler questions. An enquiry about the initiative can be done by desk research which attempts to answer the following questions:

1. What are the characteristics of this initiative?
2. Whether any previous experience of implementation is shown?
3. How might this relate to the context of implementation?

The first two questions are relatively simply explored using bibliographical search tools and resources available on the Web. These include resources available at the higher education academy and its subject centres:
www.heacademy.ac.uk/
The British Education Index (BEI, available online to subscribers), the Australian Education Index (AEI), and the North American Education Research Index Catalogue (ERIC, available free) are excellent places to begin research into specific sorts of initiatives.

1. The BEI and AEI are available at Dialogue Datastar: www.datastar-web.com
2. ERIC is available at http://searcheric.org/
3. And finally, Google Scholar is a valuable and easy resource to explore what has been written in the area of interest, including grey literature: www.scholar.google.com

The third question is most easily addressed by considering the eight moments of teaching and learning regimes in relation to the initiative.

Here the question is, what characteristics does this initiative have in relation to the moments, and how do these relate to the equivalent characteristics on the ground? In particular, the codes of signification attached to an initiative as it is received on the ground are very important, as are any effects on power relations between academics and students (or in other areas). Others of the moments may also be implicated in different ways by different initiatives. Thus, for example, the vignette on pp. 118–120 – An English Department Gets Reviewed – mentions the issue of peer-assessment by students and how such an idea was felt to be risible. In that department, that initiative would fall on stony ground for a number of reasons associated with the culture of the department and the nature and implications of student peer-assessment. The vignette on pp. 78–80 – The 'New Route' PhD at Hilltop University – shows how the discursive framing of an initiative can be very important in terms of how it is received and how it is implemented.

▶ Conclusion

Every form of research faces specific challenges, and researching for change is no different. However, the researcher who is aware of challenging issues is better able to take account of the difficulties in planning and implementing their project. One final thought, though: how the conclusions are 'read' by interested parties when the research is finished is also worth careful thought. Educational research is littered with examples of tendentious readings of research projects, especially by government departments. The Education Department's misreading of the Alexander *et al.* (1992) report on methods of teaching in primary schools is one example. Their misreading of conclusions about the 'teaching–research nexus' in universities drawn by Hattie and Marsh (1996) is only one other in a long history of such skewed interpretation. Trying to mitigate this problem by providing clear arguments, transparent presentation of data, and precisely expressed conclusions which are demonstrably based on argument and evidence is really very important. So is explicitly stating what the research does *not* show. If the practitioner-as-researcher is not in charge of any subsequent change process it is very important that he/she communicates very carefully indeed the results of the research to those who are researched.

Notes

► **Educational Ideologies**

Educational ideologies primarily revolve around three axes: the 'aim' of higher education (a liberal education or a vocational one); the important 'content' (discipline-based propositional knowledge or general transferable skills); and the important 'functions' taking place within it (research or teaching). At their most fundamental level, then, they answer the three essential questions about education: 'what exactly should we do?' 'why should we do this?' and 'how should we do it?' The literature in this area usually identifies four distinct educational ideologies which can be referred to, in shorthand, as traditionalism, progressivism, enterprise, and social reconstructionism. Traditionalism focuses on the transmission of the content of the discipline and the induction of students into it. Progressivism focuses on the development of thinking and other skills in the student, their capabilities. Enterprise sees higher education as concerning the world of work and preparing students for that. Social reconstructionism foregrounds the critical evaluation of the status quo and the capacity of research and teaching students to effect change (see Trowler, 1998, Chapter 3, for an elaboration).

1. The term 'regime' is contentious. It is not intended to suggest unconsidered compliance: political regimes are, after all, usually highly contested and unstable. The concept is elaborated in Chapter 3.
2. Critical legal studies (CLS) in the United States is very different from that in the United Kingdom. CLS in the States has been, and in some places still is, very political, and thus very divisive in departments. CLS in the United Kingdom is a minority interest, regarding itself as very radical, but largely operating outside or alongside the mainstream fairly harmoniously. British law schools have not suffered the outright warfare which has taken place in the United States.
3. The six moments are power; social relations; discourse/language; beliefs/values/desires; institutions/rituals; and material practices.

References

Åkerlind, G. S. (2007) Constraints on academics' potential for developing as a teacher. *Studies in Higher Education*, 32(1): 21–37.

Alexander, R., Rose, J., and Woodhead, C. (1992) *Curriculum Organisation and Classroom Practice in Primary Schools DES* (The Three Wise Men Report). London: DES.

Alvesson, M. (1993) *Cultural Perspectives on Organisations*. Cambridge: Cambridge University Press.

Alvesson, M. (2002) *Understanding Organizational Culture*. London: Sage.

Arthur, L. and Klapper, J. (2000) Issues and Challenges in the Teaching of Modern Languages. In C. Rust (ed.), *Improving Student Learning Through the Disciplines*. Oxford: Oxford Centre for Staff Learning and Development.

Ashwin, P. (2008) Accounting for structure and agency in 'close-up' research on teaching, learning and assessment in higher education. *International Journal of Educational Research*, 47.

Austin, A. (1998) *The Empire Strikes Back: Outsiders and the Struggle over Legal Education*. New York: New York University Press.

Bailey, F. G. (1977) *Morality and Expediency*. Oxford: Blackwell.

Bakhtin, M. M. (1981) *The Dialogical Imagination: Four Essays by M. M. Bakhtin*. M. Holquist (ed.), trans. C. Emerson and M. Holquist. Austin: University of Texas Press.

Ball, S. J. (ed.) (1990) Management as a Moral Technology – A Luddite Analysis. *Foucault and Education: Disciplines and Knowledge*. London: Routledge, pp. 153–166.

Ball, S. J. (1994) *Education Reform: A Critical and Post-Structural Approach*. Buckingham: Open University Press.

Barker, R. (ed.) (1978) *Habitats, Environments, and Human Behaviour: Studies in Ecological Psychology and Eco-Behavioural Science from the Midwest Psychological Field Station, 1947–1972*. San Francisco: Jossey Bass.

Barnett, R. (1990) *The Idea of Higher Education*. Buckingham: The Society for Research into Higher Education and Open University Press.

Barnett, R. (1994) *The Limits of Competence*. Buckingham: The Society for Research into Higher Education and Open University Press.

Barnett, R. (2000) *Realizing the University in an Age of Supercomplexity*. Buckingham: Open University Press/SRHE.

Barnett, R. and Coates, K. (2005) *Engaging the Curriculum in Higher Education*. Buckingham: Open University Press/SRHE.

Bazerman, C. (1994) *Constructing Experience*. Carbondale: Southern Illinois University Press.

Bazerman, C. (1997) Discursive restructured activities. *Mind Culture and Activity*, 4: 296–308.

Becher, T. (1988) Principles and Politics: An Interpretative Framework for University Management. In A. Westoby (ed.), *Culture and Power in Educational Organizations*. Buckingham: Open University Press/SRHE, pp. 317–328.

Becher, T. (1989) *Academic Tribes and Territories*. Buckingham: The Society for Research into Higher Education and Open University Press.

Becher, T. and Kogan, M. (eds) (1992) *Process and Structure in Higher Education*. Milton Keynes: Open University Press.

Becher, T. and Parry, S. (2005) The Endurance of the Disciplines. In I. Bleiklie and M. Henkel (eds), *Governing Knowledge*. Dordrecht: Springer, pp.133–143.

Becher, T. and Trowler, P. (2001, second edition) *Academic Tribes and Territories: Intellectual Enquiry and the Cultures of Disciplines*. Buckingham: Open University Press/SRHE.

Beckhard, R. and Pritchard, W. (1992) *Changing the Essence: The Art of Creating and Leading Fundamental Change in Organisations*. San Francisco: Jossey Bass.

Bennis, W. and Nanus, B. (1985) *Leaders*. New York: Harper Row.

Bensimon, E. M., Polkinghorne, D.E., Bauman, G. and Vallejo, E. (2004) Doing research that makes a difference. *Journal of Higher Education*, 75(1): 104–126.

Berger, P. and Luckmann, T. (1967) *The Social Construction of Reality*. Harmondsworth: Penguin (first published 1966).

Bergvall, V. (1992) *Different or Dominant? The Role of Gender in Academic Conversation*. Paper presented at the Annual Meeting of the American Educational Research Association, San Francisco, CA.

Berkenkotter, C. and Huckin, T. (1995) *Genre Knowledge in Disciplinary Communication: Cognition/Culture/Power*. New Jersey: Lawrence Erlbaum.

Bernstein, B. (1996) *Pedagogy, Symbolic Control and Identity: Theory, Research, Critique*. London: Taylor and Francis.

Berquist, W. H. (1992) *The Four Cultures of the Academy*. San Francisco: Jossey Bass.

Biggs, J. (2001) The Reflective institution: Assuring and enhancing the quality of teaching and learning. *Higher Education*, 41: 231–238.

Biglan, A. (1973a) The characteristics of subject matter in different scientific areas. *Journal of Applied Psychology*, 57(3): 195–203.

Biglan, A. (1973b) Relationships between subject matter characteristics and the structure and output of university departments. *Journal of Applied Psychology*, 57(3): 204–213.

Bloomer, M. (1997) *Curriculum Making in Post-16 Education. The Social Conditions of Studentship*. London: Routledge.

Bloomer, M. and James, D. (2001) *Cultures and Learning in Further Education*. Paper presented at the British Educational Research Association Annual Conference, University of Leeds, 13–15 September.

Blum-Kulka, S. (1997) Discourse Pragmatics. In T. Van Dijk (ed.), *Discourse as Social Interaction*. London: Sage, pp. 38–63.

Boreham, N. and Morgan, C. (2004) A sociocultural analysis of organisational learning. *Oxford Review of Education*, 30(3): 307–325.

Bourdieu, P. (1977) *Outline of a Theory of Practice*. Cambridge: Cambridge University Press.

Bourdieu, P. (1998) *Practical Reason: On the Theory of Action*. Cambridge: Polity Press.

Bourdieu, P. and Wacquant, L. J. D. (1992) *An Invitation to Reflexive Sociology*. Chicago: University of Chicago Press.

Bowe, R., Ball, S. J., and Gold, A. (1992) *Reforming Education and Changing Schools: Case Studies in Policy Sociology*. London: Routledge.

Bowker, G. and Star, S. L. (1999) *Sorting Things Out: Classification and Its Consequences*. Cambridge, MA: MIT Press.

Boyce, M. E. (2003) Organizational learning is essential to achieving and sustaining change in higher education. *Innovative Higher Education*, 28(2): 119–136.

Bradney, A. (1992) Ivory towers and satanic mills: Choices for university law schools. *Studies in Higher Education*, 17(1): 5–21.

Brown, J. S. (2005) *New Learning Environments for the 21st Century*. http://www.johnseelybrown.com/newlearning.pdf. Last accessed 12.10.07.

Brown, J. S. and Duguid, P. (1991) Organizational learning and communities of practice: Toward a unified view of working, learning and innovating. *Organization Science*, 2(1): 40–57.

Brown, J. S., Collins, A., and Duguid, P. (1989) Situated cognition and the culture of learning. *Educational Researcher*, 18: 32–42.

Burke, K. (1969) *A Grammar of Motives*. Berkely: University of California Press.

Calderhead, J. (1996) Teachers: Beliefs and knowledge. In D. Berliner and R. Calfree (eds), *Handbook of Educational Psychology*. New York: Macmillan, pp. 709–725.

Cerych, L. and Sabatier, P. (eds) (1986) *Great Expectations and Mixed Performance*. London: Trentham.

Checkland, P. and Scholes, J. (1999) *Soft Systems Methodology in Action*. Chichester: John Wiley and Sons.

Chomsky, N. (1957) *Syntactic Structures*. The Hague: Mouton & Co.

Chouliaraki, L. and Fairclough, N. (1999) *Discourse in Late Modernity: Rethinking Critical Discourse Analysis*. Edinburgh: Edinburgh University Press.

Clark, A. (1997) *Being There: Putting Brain, Body and World Together Again*. Cambridge, MA: MIT Press.

Clark, B. (1972) The organisational saga in higher education. *Administrative Science Quarterly*, 17: 178–183.

Clegg, S. C., Hardy, C., and Nord, W. (eds) (1999) *Managing Organizations: Current Issues.* London: Sage.

Cooren, F. (2004) Textual agency: How texts do things in organizational settings. *Organisation*, 11(3): 373–393.

Council for National Academic Awards (1990) *The Modular Option: Information Services Discussion Paper 5.* London: CNAA.

Cownie, F. (2004) *Legal Academics: Culture and Identities.* Oxford and Portland: Hart Publishing.

Crane, D. (1972) *Invisible Colleges: Diffusion of Knowledge in Scientific Communities.* Chicago: University of Chicago Press.

Crossman, J. (2007) The role of relationships and emotions in student perceptions of learning and assessment. *Higher Education Research and Development*, 26(3): 313–327.

Cuthbert, R. (2002) *Constructive Alignment in the World of Institutional Management.* Paper for the LTSN Generic Centre Conference: Constructive Alignment in Action. 4 November, Centre Point Conference Centre, London.

Dale, R. (1989) *The State and Education Policy.* Buckingham: Open University Press.

de Certeau, M. (1984) *The Practice of Everyday Life*, trans. S. F. Rendall. Berkeley: University of California Press.

Deal, T. E. and Kennedy, A. A. (1982) *Corporate Cultures.* Reading, MA: Addison-Wesley.

Denzin, N. (1984) *On Understanding Emotion.* San Francisco: Jossey-Bass.

Deuten, J. J. and Rip, A. (2000) Narrative infrastructure in product creation processes. *Organization*, 7(1): 69–93.

Dewey, J. (1916) *Democracy and Education.* New York: Macmillan.

Dill, D. (1999) Academic accountability and university adaptation: The architecture of an academic learning organization. *Higher Education*, 38(2): 127–154.

Dirkx, J. M. (2001) The power of feelings. Emotion, imagination and the construction of meaning in adult learning. *New Directions for Adult and Continuing Education*, 89: 63–72.

Dretske, F. (1981) *Knowledge and the Flow of Information.* Oxford: Blackwell.

Dyer, C. (1999) Researching the implementation of educational policy: a backward mapping approach. *Comparative Education*, 35(1): 45–61.

Earley, P., Evans, J., Collarbone, P., Gold, A., and Halpin, D. (2002) *Establishing the Current State of School Leadership in England.* London: DfES. http://www.dfes.gov.uk/research/programmeofresearch/projectinformation. cfm?projectid=13782&resultspage=1. Last accessed 27.10.06.

Elton, L. (2002) *Dissemination: A Change Theory Approach.* http://www. heacademy.ac.uk/resources/detail/id191_Dissemination_A_Change_Theory_ Approach. Last accessed 9.4.08.

Engestrom, Y. (2001) Expansive learning at work: Toward an activity theory reconceptualization. *Journal of Education and Work*, 14(1): 133–156.

Ensor, P. (2001) Academic programme planning in South African higher education: Three institutional case studies. In M. Breier (ed.), *Curriculum Restructuring in Higher Education in Post Apartheid South Africa*. Pretoria: CSD, pp. 85–114.

Ensor, P. (2004) Contesting discourses in higher education curriculum restructuring in South Africa. *Higher Education*, 48: 339–359.

Entwistle, N. (2007) Research into student learning and university teaching. In N. Entwistle and P. Tomlinson (eds), *Student Learning and University Teaching*. Leicester, British Journal of Educational Psychology monograph.

Entwistle, N. and Walker, P. (2002) Strategic altertness and expanded awareness in sophisticated conceptions of teaching. In N. Hativa and P. Goodyear (eds), *Teacher Thinking, Beliefs and Knowledge in Higher Education*. Dordrecht: Kluwer.

Entwistle, N., Skinner, D., Entwistle, D., and Orr, S. (2000) Conceptions and beliefs about 'Good Teaching': An integration of contrasting research areas. *Higher Education Research and Development*, 19(1): 1–16.

Eraut, M. (2000) Non-formal learning and tacit knowledge in professional work. *Journal of Educational Psychology*, 70(1): 113–136.

Eraut, M. (2000) Non-formal learning and tacit knowledge in professional work. *British Journal of Educational Psychology*, 70(1): 113–136.

Fairclough, N. (1996) Unpublished draft for talk given at AILA (Association Internationale de Linguistique Appliqué) conference. Cited in Lillis, T. M. (2001) *Student Writing: Access, Regulation, Desire*. London: Routledge, p. 49.

Fairclough, N. (1989) *Language and Power*. London: Longman.

Fanghanel, J. (2004) Capturing dissonance in university teacher education environments. *Studies in Higher Education*, 29(5): 575–590.

Farrell, J. P. (2000) Why is educational reform so difficult? *Curriculum Inquiry*, 30(1): 83–103.

Feldman, R. M. and Feldman, S. P. (2006) What links the chain: An essay on organizational remembering as practice. *Organization*, 13(6): 861–887.

Fenwick, T. J. (2004) Discursive work for educational administrators: Tensions in negotiating partnerships. *Discourse: Studies in the Cultural Politics of Education*. 25(2): 171–187.

Fish, S. (1980) *Is There a Text in This Class? The Authority of Interpretive Communities*. Cambridge, MA: Harvard University Press.

Foucault, M. (1980) *Power/Knowledge. Selected Interviews and Writings 1972–1977*. (ed. C. Gordon). New York: Pantheon Books.

Foucault, M. (1990) *The History of Sexuality Vol 1*. New York: Vintage Books.

Fox, R. (1980) *The Red Lamp of Incest*. New York: Penguin.

Fullan, M. (1999) *Change Forces: The Sequel*. London: Falmer.

Fulton, O. and Elwood, S. (1989) *Admissions to Higher Education: Policy and Practice*. Sheffield: Training Agency.

Garfinkel, H. (1967) *Studies in Ethnomethodology*. Englewood Cliffs, NJ: Prentice-Hall.

Garling, T. and Evans G. W. (eds) (1991) *Environment, Cognition and Action: An Integrated Approach*. Oxford: Oxford University Press.

Garling, T., Lindberg, E., Torell, G., and Evans, G. W. (1991) *From Environmental to Ecological Cognition*. In Garling and Evans, op cit.

Gee, J. P. (1999) *An Introduction to Discourse Analysis Theory and Method*. London: Routledge.

Geertz, C. (1983) *Local Knowledge*. New York: Basic Books.

Gerth, H. H. and Mills, C. W. (1970) *From Max Weber: Essays in Sociology*. London: Routledge and Kegan Paul (first published 1948).

Gibbons, M., Limoges, C., Nowotny, H., Schwartzman, S., Scott, P., and Trow, M. (1994) *The New Production of Knowledge: The Dynamics of Science and Research in Contemporary Societies*. London: Sage.

Gibson, J. J. (1979) *The Ecological Approach to Visual Perception*. Boston: Houghton Mifflin.

Giddens, A. (1984) *The Constitution of Society*. Cambridge: Polity Press.

Gilligan, C. (1982) *In a Different Voice: Psychological Theory and Women's Development*. Cambridge, MA and London: Harvard University Press.

Goffman, E. (1959) *The Presentation of Self in Everyday Life*. New York: Doubleday.

Goffman, E. (1961) *Encounters*. Indianapolis: Bobbs-Merrill.

Goffman, E. (1967) *Interaction Ritual*. New York: Doubleday Anchor.

Goleman, D. (1995) *Emotional Intelligence*. New York: Bantam Books.

Goleman, D. (1998) *Working with Emotional Intelligence*. New York: Bantam Books.

Gouldner, A. W. (1957) Cosmopolitans and locals: Toward an analysis of latent social roles (I and II). *Administrative Science Quarterly*, 2: 281–306, 444–480.

Grant, D., Keenoy, T., and Oswick, C. (eds) (1998) Introduction: Organizational discourse: Of diversity, dichotomy and multidisciplinarity. *Discourse and Organisation*. London: Sage, pp. 1–14.

Grieco, M. S. (1988) Birth marked? A critical view on analysing organisational culture. *Human Organisation*, 47: 84–87.

Hall, S. (1990) Cultural identity and diaspora. In J. Rutherford (ed.), *Community, Culture, Difference*. London: Lawrence and Wishart.

Halsey, A. H. (1992) *Decline of Donnish Dominion:The British Academic Professions in the Twentieth Century*. Oxford: Oxford.

Handy, C. (1993) *Understanding Organisations*. Harmondsworth: Penguin. 4th edition.

Hannan, A. and Silver, H. (2000) *Innovating in Higher Education: Teaching, Learning and Institutional Cultures*. Buckingham: Open University Press/SRHE.

Hannerz, U. (1992) *Cultural Complexity. Studies in the Social Organisation of Meaning*. New York: Columbia University Press.

Hargreaves, A. (1998) The emotional practice of teaching. *Teaching and Teacher Education*, 14(8): 835–854.

Harrington, F. J. and Turner, G. H. (2000) *Interpreting Interpreting: Studies and Reflections on Sign Language Interpreting*. Douglas McLean: Coleford.

Hart, R. A. and Conn, M. K. (1990) Developmental perspectives on decision-making and action in environments. In T. Garling and G. Evans (eds) (1991) op cit.

Harvey, D. (1996) *Justice, Nature and the Geography of Difference*. London: Blackwell.

Hattie, J. and Marsh, H. W. (1996) The relationship between research and teaching: A meta-analysis. *Review of Educational Research*, 66(4): 507–542.

Henry, C., Drew, J., Anwar, N., Benoit-Asselman, D., and Campbell, G. (1992) *EVA Project: Report of the Ethics and Values Audit*. Preston: University of Central Lancashire.

Heywood, J. (2000) *Assessment in Higher Education*. London: Jessica Kingsley.

Hickman, K. (2003) *Courtesans*. London: HarperPerennial.

Hodkinson, P. and James, D. (2003) Transforming learning cultures in further education. *Special Issue of Vocational Education & Training*, 55(4): 393–406.

Hopkins, D. (2002) *The Evolution of Strategies for Educational Change: Implications for Higher Education*. Available at http://www.heacademy.ac.uk/resources.asp?section=generic&process=search&pattern=hopkins (last accessed 15.12.06)

Hormuth, S. E. (1990) *The Ecology of the Self: Relocation and Self-concept Change*. Cambridge: Cambridge University Press.

Huber, G. P. (1991) Organizational learning: The contributing processes and the literature. *Organizational Science*, 2: 88–115.

Hull, C. (1985) Between the lines: The analysis of interview data as an exact art. *British Education Research Journal*, 11(1): 27–32.

Hutchins, E. (1995a) *Cognition in the Wild*. Cambridge, MA: MIT Press.

Hutchins, E. (1995b) How a cockpit remembers its speeds. *Cognitive Science*, 19: 265–288.

Ivanic, R. (1998) *Writing and Identity: The Discoursal Construction of Identity in Academic Writing*. Amsterdam: John Benjamins.

James, D. and Bloomer, M. (2001) *Cultures of Learning and the Learning of Cultures*. Paper presented to Cultures of Learning Conference, University of Bristol, April 2001. Available at: http://www.ex.ac.uk/education/tlc/homepage.htm. Last accessed 2.8.04.

Jarvis, P. (1999) *The Practitioner-Researcher: Developing Theory From Practice*. San Francisco: Jossey-Bass.

Jenkins, A. and Zetter, R. (2003) *Linking Research and Teaching in Departments*. http://www.heacademy.ac.uk/resources.asp?process + full_record&section=generic&id=257. Last accessed 24.1.06.

Johnson, R. W. (2006) *South Africa: The First Man, The Last Nation*. London: Phoenix (first published 2004).

Kane, R., Sandretto, S., and Heath, C. (2002) Telling half the story: A critical review of research on the teaching beliefs and practices of university academics. *Review of Educational Research*, 72(2): 177–228.

Kempner, K. (1991) Understanding cultural conflict. In W. G. Tierney (ed.), *Culture and Ideology in Higher Education*. New York: Praeger.

Kezar, A. and Eckel, P. D. (2002) The effect of institutional culture on change strategies in higher education. *Journal of Higher Education*, 73(4): 435–460.

Klein, G. A. (1989) Recognition-Primed decisions. In W. B. Rouse (ed.), *Advances in Man-Machine Systems Research*. Greenwich, CT: JAI Press, pp. 47–92.

Knight, P. and Trowler, P. (1999) It takes a village to raise a child: mentoring and the socialisation of new entrants to the academic professions. *Journal of Mentoring and Tutoring*, 7(1): 23–34.

Knight, P. and Trowler, P. R. (2001) *Departmental Leadership in Higher Education*. Buckingham: The Society for Research into Higher Education and Open University Press.

Knight, P. and Trowler, P. (2000) Department-level cultures and the improvement of learning and teaching. *Studies in Higher Education*, 25(1): 69–83.

Kolb, D. A. (1981) Learning styles and disciplinary differences. In A. Chickering (ed.), *The Modern American College*. San Francisco: Jossey Bass.

Korthagen, F. A. J. (1993) Two modes of reflection. *Teacher and Teacher Education*, 9: 317–326.

Kuh, G. D. and Whitt, E. J. (1988) *Using the Cultural Lens to Understand Faculty Behaviour*. Paper presented to the Annual Meeting of the American Educational Research Association, April 5–9.

Kuper, A. (2001) *Culture: The Anthropologist's Account*. Cambridge, MA: Harvard University Press.

Laclau, E. and Mouffee, C. (1985) *Hegemony and Socialist Strategy: Towards a Radical Democratic Politics* (trans. Moore, E. and Cammack, P.). London: Verso.

Latour, B. (2000) When things strike back: A possible contribution of 'science studies' to the social sciences. *British Journal of Sociology*, 51(1): 107–123.

Lave, J. and Wenger, E. (1991) *Situated Learning: Legitimate Peripheral Participation*. Cambridge: Cambridge University Press.

Leslie, D. W. (1996) 'Strategic governance': The wrong question? *Review of Higher Education*, 20(1): 101–112.

Levine, A. (1980) *Why Innovation Fails*. New York: State University of New York Press.

Lindsay, R., Breen, R., and Jenkins, A. (2002) Academic research and teaching quality: The views of undergraduate and postgraduate students. *Studies in Higher Education*, 27(3): 309–327.

Lipsky, M. (1980) *Street Level Bureaucracy: Dilemmas of the Individual in Public Services*. Beverley Hills: Sage Publications.

Lucas, L. (2006) *The Research Game in Academic Life*. London: SRHE/Open University Press.

Lukes, S. (2005) *Power: A Radical View*. Second edition. London: Palgrave Macmillan (first published 1974).

Mackay, N. (2001) Electoral statement. In Institute for learning and teaching in higher education (2001). *Election of 5 Members to Council Candidates' Statements*. York: ILT.

Maclean, D. (1996) Quick! Hide! Constructing a playground identity in the early weeks of school. *Language in Education*, 10 (2&3): 171–186.

Marchese, T. (1999) Foreword, In I. Hecht, M. Higgerson, W. Gmelch, and A. Tucker (eds), *The Department Chair as Academic Leader*. Phoenix: American Council on Education and Oryx Press, pp. vii–x.

Marx, K. (1852) The Eighteenth Brumaire of Louis Bonaparte. http://www.marxists.org/archive/marx/works/1852/18th-brumaire/ch01.htm. Last accessed 12.9.06.

Mathieson, S. (2004) *Report of the B.Ed Honours Interviews on the Self-Evaluation Process*. Mimeo.

McDermott, R. and Varenne, H. (1995) Culture as disability. *Anthropology and Education Quarterly*, 26(3): 324–348.

McInnis, C. (2005) The governance and management of student learning. In I. Bleiklie and M. Henkel (eds), *Governing Knowledge*. Dordrecht: Springer, pp. 81–94.

McNay, I. (1995) From collegial academy to corporate enterprise: The changing cultures of universities. In T. Schuller (ed.), *The Changing University?* Buckingham: The Society for Research into Higher Education and Open University Press, pp. 105–115.

Metzger, M. (1999) *Sign Language Interpreting:²Deconstructing the Myth of Neutrality*. Washington DC: Gallaudet University Press.

Middlehurst, R. (1997) Leadership, women and higher education. In H. Eggins (ed.), *Women as Leaders and Managers in Higher Education*. Buckingham: Open University Press/SRHE.

Miettinen, R. (1999) The riddle of things: Activity theory and actor-network theory as approaches to studying innovations. *Mind, Culture and Activity*, 6(3): 170–195.

Moore, R. (2002) *Between Covenant and Contract: Negotiating Academic Pedagogic Identities*. Presented at the Second International Basil Bernstein Symposium: Knowledges, Pedagogy and Society. Cape Town.

Moore, R. (2003) Policy driven curriculum restructuring: Academic identities in transition? In C. Prichard and P. Trowler (eds), *Realising Qualitative Research into Higher Education*. Aldershot: Ashgate.

Moore, S. and Kuol, N. (2007) Matters of the heart: Exploring the emotional dimensions of educational experience in recollected accounts of excellent teaching. *International Journal of Academic Development*, 12(2): 87–98.

Morgan-Klein, B. and Murphy, M. (2002) Access and recruitment: Institutional policy in widening participation. In P. Trowler (ed.), *Higher Education Policy and Institutional Change: Intentions and Outcomes in Turbulent Environments*. Buckingham: Open University Press/SRHE.

Nixon, J., Marks, A., Rowland, S., and Walker, M. (2001) Towards a new academic professionalism. *British Journal of Sociology of Education*, 22(2): 227–244.

O'Donovan, B., Price, M., and Rust, C. (2004) Know what I mean? Enhancing student understanding of assessment standards and criteria. *Teaching in Higher Education*, 9(3): 325–335.

Ottewill, R., Shephard, K., and Fill, K. (2002) Assessing the contribution of collections of case studies to academic development in higher education. *The International Journal for Academic Development*, 7(1): 51–62.

Ozga, J. (2000) *Policy Research in Educational Settings: Contested Terrain*. Buckingham: Open University Press.

Pajares, M. F. (1992) Teachers' beliefs and educational research: Cleaning up a messy construct. *Review of Educational Research*, 62(3): (Autumn), 307–332.

Parker, M. (2000) *Organizational Culture and Identity*. London: Sage.

Patterson, K., Grenny, J., McMillan, R., Switzler, A., and Covey, S. (2002) *Crucial Conversations: Tools for Talking When Stakes are High*. New York: McGraw-Hill.

Pendry, A. (1997) The pedagogical thinking and learning of history student teachers. In D. McItyre (ed.), *Teacher Education: Research in a New Context*. London: Paul Chapman, pp. 76–78.

Peters, T. and Waterman, R. (1982) *In Search of Excellence*. New York: Harper and Row.

Peterson, M. and Spencer, M. (1991) Understanding academic culture and climate. In M. Peterson (ed.), *ASHE Reader on Organization and Governance*. Needham Heights, MA: Simon & Schuster, pp. 140–155.

Pratt, J. and Burgess, T. (1974) *Polytechnics: A Report*. London: Pitman.

Prichard, C. (2000) *Making Managers in Universities and Colleges*. Buckingham: Open University Press/SRHE.

Prosser, M., Rickinson, M., Bence, V., Hanbury, A., and Kulej, M. (2006) *Formative Evaluation of Accredited Programmes*. York: Higher Education Academy.

Prozelytiser, P. (2000) A New Route to the PhD: A collaborative project funded by the HEFCE. Mimeo.

Reay, D. (2000) 'Dim dross?': Marginalised voices both inside and outside the academy. *Women's Studies International Forum*, 23(1): 13–21, 15.

Reay, D. (2004) Cultural capitalists and academic habitus: Classed and gendered labour in UK higher education. *Women's Studies International Forum*, 27: 31–39.

Reckwitz, A. (2002) Towards a theory of social practices: A development in culturalist theorizing. *European Journal of Social Theory*, 5(2): 243–263.

Reynolds, J. and Saunders, M. (1987) Teacher responses to curriculum policy: Beyond the 'Delivery' metaphor. In J. Calderhead (ed.), *Exploring Teachers Thinking*. London: Cassell.

Rhoades, G. (2000) Who's doing it right? Strategic activity in public research universities. *Review of Higher Education*, 24(1): 41–66.

Roberts, K. H., Stout, S. K., and Halpern, J. J. (1994) Decision dynamics in two highly reliable military organizations. *Management Science*, 40(5): 614–624.

Robertson, D. (1994) *Choosing to Change*. London: HEQC.

Rodriguez, H. (1998) *Activity Theory and Cognitive Sciences*. http://http://www.nada.kth.se/~henrry/papers/ActivityTheory.html. Last accessed 02.08.06.

Rogoff, B. (2003) *The Cultural Nature of Human Development*. Oxford: Oxford University Press.

Rommetveit, R. (1979) *The Role of Language in the Creation and Transmission of Social Representations*. Unpublished manuscript. Quoted in Wertsch, 1998, p. 112.

Schutz, A. and Luckmann, T. (1989) *The Structures of the Life-World*. Northwestern University Press (first published 1973).

Scott, P. (1995) *The Meanings of Mass Higher Education*. Buckingham: SRHE and Open University Press.

Seel, R. (2000), Complexity and culture: New perspectives on organisational change. *Organisations & People*, 7(2): 2–9. (Also at http://www.newparadigm.co.uk/culture-complex.htm. Last accessed 16.12.06)

Seierstad, A. (2004) *The Bookseller of Kabul*. London: Virago.

Senge, P. (1990) *The Fifth Discipline*. New York: Doubleday.

Shay, S. B. (2003) *The Assessment of Undergraduate Final Year Projects: A Study of Academic Professional Judgement*. Unpublished PhD thesis University of Cape Town, 2003.

Shay, S. B. (2004) The assessment of complex performance: A socially-situated interpretive act. *Harvard Educational Review*, 74(3): 307–329.

Shils, E. (1981) *Tradition*. Chicago, IL: University of Chicago Press.

Shove, E., Watson, M., Hand, M., and Ingram, J. (2007) *The Design of Everyday Life*. Oxford: Berg.

Sinnott, J. and Johnson, L. (1996) Reinventing the University. Norwood, NJ: Ablex.

Skelton, A. (2004) Understanding 'teaching excellence' in higher education: A critical evaluation of the national teaching fellowships scheme. *Studies in Higher Education*, 29(4): 451–468.

Smith, M. J. (2000) *Culture: Reinventing the Social Sciences*. Buckingham: Open University Press.

Smith, N. (ed.) (1982) *Mutual Knowledge*. New York & London: Academic Press.

Snaith, I. (1990) Company law on degree courses: Survey report. *Company Lawyer*, 11(9): 177–183.

Stenhouse, L. (1979) *The Problem of Standards in Illuminative Research*. Lecture given at the Annual General Meeting of the Scottish Educational Research Association, Glasgow: University of Glasgow, mimeo cited in C. Hull (1985) op cit.

Stevenson, R. B. (2004) Constructing knowledge of educational practices from case studies. *Environmental Education Research*, 10(1): 39–51.

Still, A. and Costall, A. (1989) Mutual elimination of dualism. In L. S. Vygotsky and J. J. Gibson (eds), *Quarterly Newsletter of the Laboratory of Comparative Human Cognition*, 2(4): 131–136.

Sugrue, C. (1997) Student teachers' lay theories and teaching identities: Their implications for professional development. *European Journal of Teacher Education*, 20: 213–225.

Svensson, L. (ed.) (1998) *Meeting Rivers: A Report on Transnational Cultural Flows and National Cultural Processes*. Lund: Lund University Press.

Taylor, J. (2006) 'Big is beautiful.' Organisational change in the universities in the United Kingdom: New models of institutional management and the changing role of academic staff. *Higher Education in Europe*, 31(3): 251–273.

Temple, P. (2007) *Learning Spaces for the 21st Century: A Review of the Literature*. York: Higher Education Academy.

Tierney, W. (1987) The semiotic aspects of leadership: An ethnographic perspective. *American Journal of Semiotics*, 5: 233–250.

Tierney, W. G. (1988) Organisational culture in higher education. *Journal of Higher Education*, 59, 1: 2–21.

Tight, M. (2004) Research into higher education: An a-theoretical community of practice? *Higher Education Research and Development*, 23(4): 395–411.

Tillema, H. H. (1997) Stability and change in student teachers beliefs. *European Journal of Teacher Education*, 20: 209–212.

Trowler, P. and Knight, P. (1999) Organizational socialization and induction in universities: Reconceptualizing theory and practice. *Higher Education*, 37: 177–195.

Trowler, P. (1996) Angels in marble?: Accrediting prior experiential learning in higher education. *Studies in Higher Education*, 21(1): 17–31.

Trowler, P. (1998) *Academics Responding to Change: New Higher Education Frameworks and Academic Cultures*. Buckingham: Open University Press/SRHE.

Trowler, P. (2001) Captured by the discourse? The socially constitutive power of new higher education discourse in the UK. *Organization*, 8(2): 183–201.

Trowler, P. and Bamber, V. (2005) Compulsory higher education teacher education: Joined-up policies; institutional architectures; enhancement cultures. *International Journal for Academic Development*, 10(2): 79–93.

Trowler, P. and Cooper, A. (2002) Teaching and learning regimes: Implicit theories and recurrent practices in the enhancement of teaching and learning through educational development programmes. *Higher Education Research and Development*, 21(3): 221–240.

Trowler, P. and Knight, P. (2000) Coming to know in higher education: Theorising faculty entry to new work contexts. *Higher Education Research and Development*, 19(1): 27–42.

Trowler, P. and Knight, P. (2001) *Exploring the Implementation Gap: Theory and Practices in Change Interventions*. In P. Trowler (ed.), *Higher Education Policy and Institutional Change*. Buckingham: Open University Press/SRHE.

Trowler, P. and Turner, G. (2002) Exploring the hermeneutic foundations of university life: Deaf academics in a hybrid community of practice. *Higher Education*, 43: 227–256.

Trowler, P., Fanghanel, J., and Wareham, T. (2005) Freeing the chi of change: The higher education academy and enhancing teaching and learning in higher education. *Studies in Higher Education*, 30(5): 427–444.

Trowler, P., Saunders, M., and Knight, P. (2002) *Change Thinking, Change Practices: A Guide to Change for Heads of Department, Subject Centres and Others Who Work Middle-Out*. Report for the Learning and Teaching Support Network, Generic Centre. http://www.heacademy.ac.uk/resources/detail/ourwork/institutions/Change_Academy_Essential_Reading. Last accessed 29.4.08.

Tushnet, M. (1990) Critical legal studies: A political history. *The Yale Law Journal*, 100: 1515–1544.

Tyack, D. and Cuban, L. (1995) *Tinkering Towards Utopia: A Century of Public School Reform*. Cambridge, MA, London: Harvard University Press.

Van Maanen, J. and Kunda, G. (1989) 'Real feelings': Emotional expression and organizational culture. *Research in Organizational Behavior*, 11: 43–103.

Vaughan, D. (1996) *The Challenger Launch Decision: Risky Technology, Culture and Deviance at NASA*. Chicago: University of Chicago Press.

Wadensjo, C. (1998) *Interpreting as Interaction*. London: Longman.

Warner, D. and Palfreyman, D. (2003) *Managing Crisis*. Maidenhead: Open University Press.

Warwick (2007a) Reinvention Centre for Undergraduate Education http:// www2.warwick.ac.uk/fac/soc/sociology/rsw/current/reinvention. Last accessed 9.4.08

Warwick (2007b) The Reinvention Centre at Westwood. http://www2.warwick.ac.uk/fac/soc/sociology/research/cetl/westwood/ (accessed 4.10.07)

Watson, D. (1989) *Managing the Modular Course: Perspectives from Oxford Polytechnic*. Buckingham: Open University Press/SRHE.

Wenger, E. (1998) *Communities of Practice: Learning, Meaning and Identity*. Cambridge: Cambridge University Press.

Wenger, E. (2000) Communities of practice and social learning systems. *Organization*, 7(2): 225–246.

Wenger, E., McDermott, R., and Snyder, W. (2002) *Cultivating Communities of Practice*. Boston, MA: Harvard Business School Press.

Wertsch, J. V. (1998) *Mind as Action*. Oxford: Oxford University Press.

Wertsch, J. W. (1991) *Voices of the Mind: A Sociocultural Approach to Mediated Action*. London: Harvester Wheatsheaf.

Whitcomb, D. B. and Deshler, D. (1983) *The Values Inventory: A Process for Clarifying Institutional Culture*. EDRS document number ED 254, 113.

Willmott, H. (1993) Strength is ignorance; slavery is freedom: Managing culture in modern organizations. *Journal of Management Studies*, 30(4): 515–552.

Winberg, C. (2003) Language, content and context in the education of architects. In R. Wilkinson (ed.), *Integrating Content and Language: Meeting the Challenge of Multilingual Higher Education*. Maastricht: University of Maastricht Press, pp. 320–332.

Wittgenstein, L. (1982) *Last Writings on the Philosophy of Psychology*. (C. G. Luckhardt and M. A. E. Aue, trans.) Oxford: Blackwell (originally published, 1948).

Woodrow, M. (1993) Franchising: The quiet revolution. *Higher Education Quarterly*, 47(3): 207–220.

Wright, S. (2002) *A Discipline Specific Educational Development Programme for Anthropology*. Final Report to FDTL.

Wuthnow, R., Hunter, J. D., and Bergeson, A. (1987) *Cultural Analysis. The work of Peter L. Berger, Mary Douglas, Michelle Foucault and Jurgen Habermas*. London: Routledge and Kegan Paul.

Index